Who Sees When
The Heart
Cries

Barbara A Hayes

Who Sees When The Heart Cries
Copyright © 2019 by Barbara A Hayes
All rights reserved. No part of this publication may be reproduced, distributed, or transmitted in any form or by any means, including photocopying, recording, or other electronic or mechanical methods, without the prior written permission of the author, except in the case of brief quotations embodied in critical reviews and certain other non-commercial uses permitted by copyright law.

Tellwell Talent
www.tellwell.ca
ISBN
978-0-2288-0341-6 (Paperback)

Charm is deceptive, and beauty is vain; but a woman who fears the LORD, is to be praised. Proverbs 31:30 (NIV).

Dedication

This book is dedicated to my wonderful children. You always believe in me and believe I can do anything I put my mind to. Thank you for your love and support. We have struggled through many hardships, and there were times we cried together and laughed together. You are the reason I am writing this book.

To my beautiful grandchildren, who give me so much love, I am truly blessed. To my loving mom, you left this earthly home at a young age for your heavenly home. The times you traveled on your knees, your prayers were not in vain. Your love and support have made me the woman I am today. My brother, the suffering you went through before you left this world cannot be compared with the blessings that awaited you in heaven. You endured to the end.

Save the best for last, yet first, to my wonderful Savior and Lord Jesus Christ who has shed his precious blood for me. When I have fallen, you have picked me up and given me your grace and strength in every difficult situation I have faced. You are my heartbeat. My desire is to love and serve you, all the days of my life. All glory, honor and praise be unto you!

Table of Contents

Foreword ix
Acknowledgements xi
Introduction xiii

Chapter 1   Grenada, My Homeland 1
Chapter 2   Airplanes Bring Babies 2
Chapter 3   Five-Year-Old Memorizing the Bible 4
Chapter 4   Grandma's Homemade Bread 6
Chapter 5   Christmas Exciting! 8
Chapter 6   Canada, Here I Come! 9
Chapter 7   Canada: Christmas 2000 11
Chapter 8   I Need to Write God a Letter 13
Chapter 9   Man With Mask 16
Chapter 10 Child Molester 17
Chapter 11 My Pity Party 19
Chapter 12 Escaped Kidnap 24
Chapter 13 Migration to Trinidad 25
Chapter 14 Returning to Grenada 27
Chapter 15 The Teacher Asked Me Out on A Date 29
Chapter 16 Shock Cured His Asthma 31
Chapter 17 Hit by Bus 33
Chapter 18 The Guilt Trip 34
Chapter 19 The Hardest Decision 37
Chapter 20 Was It a Nightmare? 38
Chapter 21 I Couldn't Believe I Failed 39
Chapter 22 Two Girls Want to Be Nurses 41
Chapter 23 Bikini Contest 43

Chapter 24 Trinidad	44
Chapter 25 Grenada: A Day of Horror	46
Chapter 26 Cuban Bone Specialists Disappointed	49
Chapter 27 Jealousy Rejoices Hope Wins	52
Chapter 28 My Malnourished Son	54
Chapter 29 How I Met My Husband	55
Chapter 30 Ignoring the Signs	57
Chapter 31 Waiting Was Hard	62
Chapter 32 Immigration	65
Chapter 33 Question by My Five-Year-Old	66
Chapter 34 Reaching Out for Help	69
Chapter 35 Child Molester in the School	73
Chapter 36 I Thought He was Sent by God	79
Chapter 37 The Journey of a Single Parent	83
Chapter 38 Who is That Woman in the Mirror?	89
Chapter 39 The Couch Became My Best Friend	90
Chapter 40 Life Controlled by Fear	92
Chapter 41 Grenada: 1983 Invasion	97
Chapter 42 Watch out for the Boys	98
Chapter 43 Afraid to Be Happy	100
Chapter 44 Not Her Fault	102
Chapter 45 Get Over It	104
Chapter 46 Enough is Enough	106
Chapter 47 When Communication Breaks Down	107
Chapter 48 Slipping Back	109
Chapter 49 Taking Authority	111
Chapter 50 Know Your Self Worth	113
Chapter 51 Healing is a Process Not a Product	118
Chapter 52 My Vision	122
Chapter 53 Breaking in The Shaping	125
Chapter 54 Innocent Pays for The Guilt	127
Chapter 55 Broken in Use?	129
Chapter 56 You Never Know Who Is Watching	133
Chapter 57 The Thorn and the Nails	136
Chapter 58 God Sent You Just in Time	138
Chapter 59 Spreading the Word	139

Chapter 60	God Turns it Around for Good	141
Chapter 61	Know Your Enemy	143
Chapter 62	Finding What Works for You	145
Chapter 63	Kneeling at the Cross	150
Chapter 64	Respecting Each Other.	157
Chapter 65	Don't Allow What's in the Rearview Mirror to Scare You	161
Chapter 66	Be A Woman Not a Woe 'man	167
Chapter 67	Know Your Purpose	172
Chapter 68	Self-Evaluation	175
Chapter 69	Preparation for Exaltation	178
Chapter 70	God is Still in Control	181
Chapter 71	Time to Get Rid of The Crutch	186

Foreword

Many people have learned from their experiences, and in turn have helped others. Life is a journey, and many of us are in the boat. When the tide rises we look for something to hold on to. I never thought I would be writing a book today. I have taken it as an opportunity to share some of my experiences: the good, the bad, and the ugly most of us encounter in our lives, in the hopes that this book can help protect others from repeatedly making the same mistakes.

I remember writing a paragraph about riding on life train, just a few days after my mom lost her battle with breast cancer in 1987. I realized writing had become a form of therapy for me, while I worked through the question imbedded in my mind: "Why didn't God heal my mom?" She was a strong Christian woman with great faith, who believed she would be healed and have a street ministry to share the good news of what the Lord had done for her. She hoped those who heard her testimony would be stirred in their faith, and by doing so, it would also bring hope to the hopeless. Unfortunately, that was not to be, and that left me feeling confused. "Why didn't God heal her?" There are people who live to be a good old age, over ninety and over a hundred, and I sometimes wondered, "Why couldn't my mom live to see a good old age like that?"

I remember my sister locked herself in her room and cried for hours when my mom died. There are so many things in life we may not understand, and many of our questions may go unanswered, but one thing is for sure: God is still on the throne, still in control, and he cares about each and every one of us. It is never too late to make a turnaround in our lives. There is always hope for the hopeless. Also, whatever the enemy intends for bad, God will turn around for good. I have experienced this in my life, as have many others, and we can testify to it. We must continue to hold fast to the word of God. Some give up when the going gets tough, but what we must understand is that we cannot keep ourselves. *"God is our keeper."* See Psalms 121:5. (KJV.)

Acknowledgements

Sincere thanks to Pastor Raymond Cyrus of Open Heaven Ministries in Scarborough, Ontario, for your mentoring and the prophecies you have spoken throughout my life. I can see they are all unfolding. Thank you for believing in me and giving me the opportunity to preach at Open Heaven Ministries on Ladies' Sunday. What a wonderful time we had in the presence of the Lord! Many people rededicated their lives to Jesus Christ, and the Holy Spirit was in full control. The enemy was angry because he had lost. He had a plan to put me in bondage, but God's plan is bigger and greater! I thank God for the ministry he has called me to, where I can make a difference in the lives of others. I am blessed to be a blessing. Thank you, pastor, for your prayers and encouragement.

To Pastor Richard of the Mountain of Fire Ministries in Etobicoke, Ontario. Thank you for taking the time to lend a listening ear when I needed it and thank you for your counselling and prayer. You are truly a blessing.

To Pastor Olu and Vicki David of the Intercultural Worship Centre, thank you for your prayer and support, and for being a friend when I needed someone to talk to. You are all great people, and it is such a blessing and privilege to be part of the family of God with you, working together and looking out for each other.

Introduction

I believe if we were given the opportunity to go back into our past to correct our mistakes, we would not hesitate. I am a living example of my words. I have learned to pull strength from my weakest moments and have continued to stay strong through God's grace. God has pulled me from suffocating situations and uncontrollable emotions, that were holding me back from many opportunities. Most of us go on a guilt trip because of disappointments and hurts which have resulted in regrets and pain.

I have met people struggling with guilt, fear, and emotional turmoil, who are just existing, not living. There are people who have lost their self-esteem, and some are emotionally crippled because they have suffered various abuses. For that reason, they have become afraid to trust anyone. Some people never acknowledge the pain until they find themselves in a relationship. Some are so hurt they cannot even talk about it. Sad to say, people end up in a mental institution, while some are the living example of their past situation. Most of us look good on the outside yet are crying on the inside. Sometimes emotional pain can disfigure a person's face and cause them to look like they are carrying the world on their shoulders. There is a saying that a person's eyes never lie. There are those who smile through their tears, and if you talk with them for five minutes, they will start telling you their story. Emotional pain can silently destroy a person if it is not taken care of, and when people do not know how to deal with these issues they sink into deep depression.

Some people just need a listening ear. A few years ago, a lady came in to do some shopping in the store where I was working. I approached her and asked her how she was doing. The way she was staring at me I could tell something was not quite right. It was obvious she wanted to talk about it and she immediately began to pour her heart out. She said, "I am very upset because of what my husband did to me and my children. He left me for a younger woman and doesn't want to have anything to do with me or the children. I am now a broken woman." I could tell by the tone of her voice that her emotions were taking control, and the pain she was feeling was quite intense. A beautiful woman, walking around with emotional pain from a deep emotional wound, just hoping to find someone who would lend her a listening ear. I felt sorry for this lady, and all I could say to her was, "I understand what you are going through, and I will keep you in my prayers." She thanked me and went about her business.

Writing a manuscript like this is not the easiest thing. In the process it awakes the pain of painful memories, that many people cannot deal with. It takes a lot of courage. Hats off to those of us who have taken the time and courage to invite the world into our closet. Through many books, and self-help books, people have used their experiences to help others and give them the chance to come out of their own closets. They have been given a voice, which brings them hope and a chance to become a better person on this planet. People need to talk, and some are just waiting to break the silence. I must let you know that God had you in mind when he placed it on my heart to write this book.

The Danger of Emotional Pain

Emotional pain can cause some mental disorders, and some people are like a ticking bomb; you do not want to rush them too much. Many people express their feelings through anger. Emotional pain can also cause health issues and instability. For many years, I walked around smiling and pretending to be happy like everything was good, until one day reality hit me. I could hear that voice saying to me that I needed to admit my feelings, that I could not continue like that. I was just a broken person trying to keep the pieces together.

There are people who try hard to keep it together, until it becomes uncontrollable. We must realize for us to get help, we must reach out for help. We cannot function properly while holding onto emotional pain. The mask most people have been wearing for years is so old, that others can now see through the creases. It is time to rip it off. The time for pretending has passed, and this is a new day. I want to let you know, that this book you are now holding in your hands, it is God's way of reaching out to you, and telling you how much he loves you and cares about you. He knows what you are going through, and he wants to deliver you and set you free, so that you can get on with your life and live the life that he has died for you to live.

As the psalmist David wrote. *"This is the day that the Lord has made. We will rejoice and be glad in it"* (Psalm 118:24 KJV).

It is a choice we must make ourselves. Every day is an opportunity the Lord has given us to make changes in our lives. We cannot allow the enemy to continue beating the drums and laughing. Jesus promised us healing. He would never go back on his word. In this book you will learn to take hold of life before it passes you by, and today could be your day. When I was a child I remember my cousin had a story book that we loved to read. On one of the pages was a picture of an old woman with a crooked nose and a black pointed straw hat, riding on a broom with a long black gown. She had magical powers. I came to realize it was all a fairy tale.

How we treat someone defines the person that we really are, and we must be careful to avoid residual Karma.

Chapter 1

Grenada, My Homeland

I was born on the beautiful Island of Grenada, known as the Isle of Spice, and grew up in a small village in the parish of Saint David. My mom was a single parent. She raised all three of her children on her own. I do not know how she would have done it without the grace of God.

I can still remember those nights when she would get out of bed, losing sleep, heat water over a kerosene lamp to make me tea, and then sing me a lullaby as she rocked me back to bed. She would rub lamp oil on my stomach to ease those terrible stomach cramps. I do not believe it was the lamp oil that healed the stomach aches. I believe it was her warm, gentle hands.

Mothers have that warm touch that no child could experience from anyone else. Nothing can take the place of a mother's love. I don't think any of us have lost the memories of our childhood days. Although I am a grown woman now, I still remember numerous things from when I was a child. I remember seeing children in the neighborhood tying out sheep and goats. I used to wish I had one myself. I would take a piece of wood and tie it on a string, drag it and pretend I was tying out my sheep. I chased butterflies, played dollhouse and hide and seek with my cousins in the moonlight. That was the best, and a whole lot of fun. Wait 'til you hear the rest.

Chapter 2

Airplanes Bring Babies

I asked where babies came from. The answer I got was the airplane drops them off. It confused my little mind, and left me wondering, "How can an airplane drop off a baby?" It just did not seem to make sense and trying to figure it out created more confusion in me. Yet, I would get so excited whenever I saw or heard an airplane. I would start shouting at the top of my voice, "Airplane! Please bring a baby for me!" I was too innocent to know or think that it takes a male and a female to have a baby. Nowadays, you cannot fool children with that, but at that time it made sense to my parents to hide the truth from us until we got older.

My mom was a seamstress, sewing for a couple people in the neighborhood, only charging five and ten dollars for a dress. Even though that was a good price, it was not too often she would get work. I never heard her complain of having to parent on her own, at any time though. I had thick, long hair, and when mother combed it her hands would get tired, to the point where she would feel a sensation like pins and needles running through them. She would stop for a minute, tap her hands on her legs, and continue.

Matching ribbons, dresses with sashes, matching socks and shoes, she took pride in dressing her little girl. I was a happy little girl with no care about the world, just eat, play, dress and look pretty. I was the brown girl in the ring and enjoyed dancing my hula-hoop and playing ringer roses.

On a rainy day the children in the neighborhood loved to go out and play barefoot. I would gaze out the window, wishing I could do the same. A couple of times, unknown to my parents, I snuck out of the house and followed my cousin Marg down to the river. Marg and I used to love jumping river stones and catching crayfish. I knew it was not the right thing to sneak out of the house, but I also knew if I had asked my parents, the answer would have been, "No."

When I would get caught coming home, mom would make sure I ate first, and then, when I would think she had forgotten all about it, she would quietly pull out the strap and warp my little behind. She taught us children to be loving and caring and to respect everyone, down to the smallest child. For instance, the evening I came home from school with an extra pencil that did not belong to me, she asked where I had gotten it. I told her I had borrowed it from a child in the class. She would say to me, make sure you take it back to the child the next morning when you leave for school.

Chapter 3
Five-Year-Old Memorizing the Bible

I remember my younger sister, at five years old, attended a private school owned by a Seventh Day Adventist lady, just about fifteen minutes walking distance from where we lived. Every evening when my sister came home from school, she would tell us she had to learn the books of the bible for homework. Listening to her memorizing the books of the bible, all by herself, was just amazing! I do not think I could have done it that well.

My grandmother was a housewife and worked in the kitchen from morning until she was ready to go to bed. My grandfather used to plant a large garden, raise chickens, and take care of cows and pigs. Most mornings he would draw milk from the cow, and she would boil it with cinnamon and green lime peel. It would taste amazing. They all depended on the garden to get by most of the time, and every so often, my grandmother would check to see if the hens had laid any eggs. One egg would be shared among a household of seven. There were times when she would put a pot of water on the fire, not knowing where the next meal would be coming from, but even so, I cannot remember any of us going to bed hungry.

We were quite fortunate to have fruit trees. We took advantage of the nice juicy mangoes, and I used to love climbing the plum trees and shaking down the plums. My parents never let us go back to school without giving us a dose of castor oil. It was what they called a washout after a long vacation, and it was a way of cleansing our systems after all the mangoes we had feasted on. Another gag was cod-liver oil every morning. That habit has stuck with me, and I now consider it the best fish oil. In the moonlight, we would sit on the house step, tell riddles and play guessing games. Those were the good old days.

Chapter 4

Grandma's Homemade Bread

The sweet aroma from Grandma's homemade bread, that she baked every Saturday, spread right throughout the neighborhood. We could not wait for it to come out of the oven, so we could dab some salt-butter on and just enjoy. We knew the blessing of contentment and realized it was not about having steak and potatoes with garden salad or rice and peas with stew fish every day that makes a person happy. There were days when all we had was a couple of steamed green bananas and a cup of hot chocolate tea for breakfast, and we were happy. Some children have so much to eat they do not know what to choose, so with that they complain there is nothing to eat, and so much food gets wasted. We had nothing to waste.

We never knew anything about washing machines or dryers. My mom used to take the clothes to the river and wash them, while I sat on the river stone and caught crayfish. In time, she was able to run a water pipe outside of the house, so we could do our laundry at home instead of going to the river. Before we were able to purchase a kerosene stove, coal pot and firewood was the thing. It was fun blowing the firewood until it blazes. My little cheek would hurt, and my eyes would run water from the smoke. We lived on a hill, where it was difficult at times for us to get water during the day, but water would come at nights and we would fill all the buckets and catch enough to last throughout the day. I remember the day my uncle brought home a fridge and a television, I felt like we were the rich people on the hill. Never mind that when the rain fell it was something else.

It was a muddy hill, so when rain fell you can just imagine what it was like. When I dressed to go out or to work, I had a purse in one hand and dress shoes in the other, so I could change shoes at the bottom of the hill. Sometimes the bus would be waiting, while I took off my muddy shoes. To me, it was embarrassing at times, especially when the bus was coming, and I'm trying to run down the hill in the mud with boots much bigger than my feet, I could hardly lift it as it would get so heavy with the amount of mud stuck under it. The worst was when I would fall and get my clothes dirty. Then, I would have to go back and change. Sometimes, instead of getting upset, I would have a good laugh at myself.

Chapter 5

Christmas Exciting!

We loved celebrating Christmas. It was always an exciting time for us. I remember one Christmas Day, the mother of one of my cousins surprised me with a doll. It was the cutest doll, and the only time I could see and play with it was on Christmas Day, since as soon as the day was over, my mom would hide it away until the next Christmas. I think it was funny, when she would sneak the same doll into a sock hanging behind the bedroom door, pretending Santa dropped by. As children we hadn't the luxury that some children had, but we were quite happy and contented with whatever little we had.

When I became a teenager, Mom taught me how to sew the curtains and cushion cases for the living room. I loved decorating the house and putting up the Christmas tree, while listening to the Christmas songs playing on the radio and my mother and grandmother in the kitchen cooking ham, boiling sorrel, and making the best ginger beer ever. My aunt would show up with delicious fruit cake and we all would have a great time. We celebrated Christmas the good old-fashioned way. We enjoyed going from door to door sharing cake, with a glass of ginger beer or sorrel with the neighbors, and wishing them a merry Christmas.

Chapter 6

Canada, Here I Come!

Nineteen eighty-seven was quite a rough year. I lost my grandmother in the month of October, while I was on my way to Canada, after spending a few weeks with my cousin in Trinidad. At that time, my mom went over to Grenada to visit her as she was very ill. And when my mother returned to Canada, two months later, she also went home to be with the Lord. That was December 17th, 1987, the same day as my oldest daughter's birthday, and one day before my birthday. What a year.

A lot had happened in that year. My husband and I had decided to go our separate ways. I just could not believe all this was happening. It was a trying time. It was like one hit after the next.

My mom was residing in Canada, and with her help, I was fortunate to come to this beautiful country. It was a relief from my abusive husband, but I had to leave my children behind; I had no choice. I knew I wanted to make a better life for them and myself, and to do that I had to take the risk. It was not the easiest thing to do, and I must indeed say it took a lot of courage. Sometimes you get to that place where you have to say enough is enough, and that life offers more than you would settle for, even if you don't know what is behind the curtain, or what lies ahead. I have experienced some pitfalls along the way, which brought me a lot of pain. I must say life is indeed a learning experience that shapes us into the person we become. Life is about taking chances, which is not always the easiest thing. There are many things that we may try to avoid, but there are times when we need to do what we think is best for us and our love ones. We must also weigh the pros and the cons.

Chapter 7

Canada: Christmas 2000

In the year 2000, I was sinking into a deep depression. It made it difficult for me to enjoy the season I usually looked forward to. My children were still young, and I thought it was unfair to rob them of the Christmas joy all children look forward to, and that only comes once a year. And, of course, children are excited to open their presents. I had to find the strength to force myself out of the house to get them a little something that would light up their little faces and bring joy to their hearts.

With my emotions getting the best of me, I looked at other people who all looked quite happy, busily enjoying the season, shopping in the malls with bright smiles on their faces. In my mind I was asking, why can't I enjoy myself and be happy as them. At that moment, I could hear a voice saying to me, "You are not alone. There are many people just like you, and you need to say a prayer for them." I knew it was no one else, but God talking to me. I paused for a moment and prayed for the lonely, the sad, the sick, and the broken-hearted.

God always reminds us there are others in the same boat with us or even worse off than us. If we only take the time to reflect for a moment and consider others, even in our brokenness, we can perhaps save a life. This would not only help us to feel better about ourselves, but it would also help us to change our focus, thereby speeding up the healing process and lessening our pain. There's always another person that is singing your song. You would think after praying it got better, No, it did not, but at least I felt a bit of relief for the moment. As time went by it got worse.

Chapter 8

I Need to Write God a Letter

After praying and not seeing results, I became frustrated. I thought if I wrote God a letter he would answer quickly.

"Dear God," I wrote. "I am feeling helpless and hopeless. I am broken to the point where I do not think I can be fixed. I feel like I am just existing and not living. Please, God, I need you to help me! I need a miracle in my life. My children need me, and they are not happy seeing me unhappy. I know I always ask you to use me, but I did not realize I would be going through this state of feeling broken. I guess you cannot use something unless it is first broken. I feel like I am down in the valley. I am very unhappy. I prefer to be on the mountain top."

I cannot say God answered my letter right away. I knew I had to wait on His own timing, but in the waiting process he gave me his grace. Many times, if we are going through a situation or dark period in our lives that seems unreasonable and we do not know where to turn, the only person we can turn to is Jesus. He promised he would never leave us nor forsake us (Hebrews 13:5). Whether we believe it or not, he will remain true to his word.

Natures Beauty

Whenever I needed a quiet time with the Lord, I would escape to the park with a pen and my bible and find my favorite tree. I would sit under it for hours and cry out to God. After a while I could hear his gentle voice, as he whispered in my ears. "Be still and know that I am God."

The birds flocking together sang beautifully. The butterflies that stopped by to smell the roses were just amazing to see. I listened to the rustling of the branches on the trees and admired those colorful leaves. The blue skies were parched with gray and white with a ray of sunlight between. Thank you Lord! There is always a silver lining behind the dark clouds. At that moment I felt the peace of God come over me. I dropped on my knees. As the pain begin to cease, I lifted my hands in worship and praise to the Creator.

I then opened my bible and ran into the scripture that Jesus prayed for me before I was born. I was in awe! "Lord you prayed for me before I was born? Wow!" I thought. This amazed me. He already knew what I would encounter in this world and had it all under control. Nothing is surprising to him. I prayed and asked Him to please send me a good lady friend who I could walk with and go driving with sometimes. That prayer was answered the quickest. One day, on my nature walk at the park, I ran into a lady and her beautiful daughter. I decided to strike up a conversation, so I said, "What a beautiful day this is. Isn't God good?" She replied, "Yes, God is great!" I went up to her and said my name is Barbara. In turn she introduced herself and her daughter. She told me her name was Joan, that she was a nurse, and a Seventh-day Adventist. Surprisingly, I learned that she lived in the building across from me. We chatted for a while, and she invited me to her house one day. I met her mom and from there we became good friends. Joan and I prayed together, I visited her church and there were times she invited me for a sleepover. Her mom was a wonderful person too. She loved making bread pudding, and she would always make sure to keep some for me. After a while, my friend Joan moved to a different town, and months after that, I moved to a different place too. We stayed in touch by email. I knew God had set up that meeting with Joan and me that day at the park. God connects us to the right people in the right time.

In times when you are sad and broken, you become weak, you

feel that all your strength is gone and you have no energy to go on, you have lost your zeal to do things that you always wanted to do.

> Proverbs 17:22 *tells us, A merry heart doeth good like medicine but, a broken spirit dries the bone*s."

How many people including Christians are not enjoying their lives, which is sad, and when we are not enjoying our lives, satan is glad to make a mockery of us. *"Jesus tells us that the thief come to kill and destroy, but he come to give life" (John 10:10).*

We should ask ourselves the question, why aren't we enjoying life to its fullest. We look around and see the people of the world enjoying theirs, and we begin to think and feel that God has forsaken us.

Chapter 9

Man With Mask

Grenada
Carnival in Grenada is a time most people look forward to. Some memories, good or bad, stay with us forever. I was only eight years old, when a man from my neighborhood, disguised in a mask, climbed up to my window to frighten me. He thought it was funny, but I think it was selfish, and it was a terrible thing to do to a child. I knew who he was, but I was still terrified. I dreaded the mask. I could feel my little heart racing, but not for hell would this man stop. He enjoyed seeing me infuriated. In my mind, I wondered how someone could be so heartless.

I cried my little heart out, and I pranced around my mom in terror. The more my mom pleaded with him to stop, the more he kept going. Some people do not understand how much something like that can affect a child psychologically. Many years have rolled by, but, when I think about it, I sometimes feel like it is happening all over again. This could be one of the reasons why some children, when they grow up, become emotionally disturbed or experience anxiety that makes it difficult for them to function normally.

Chapter 10

Child Molester

At the age of eight, I was sexually molested by a twenty-one-year-old man that one of my uncles brought home to live with us for a couple of days. He felt sorry for the young man because he had just moved in with his uncle, not far from where we lived, and for some reason he and his uncle were not getting along. My uncle reached out to help him, but little did he know he was bringing a child molester to our house. I was just an innocent eight-year-old girl sitting on the doorstep, playing with my little puppy, when he lifted me up and sat me on his lap, working his finger up my private area. My mother and grandmother were in the kitchen making dinner and they had no idea what was going on.

I never said anything to my uncle nor any of them about it. I was too innocent to understand what was going on. I do not understand what kind of pleasure a man can get from sexually molesting a child. I believe that I was robbed of my innocence. I cannot say it affected me back then, because I was still able to function as a child and play and do childish things. Now that I'm an adult, I realize how much I was taken advantage of even though it was just for that one minute.

Some people are still suffering today, all because of this terrible experience. Not being able to talk about it is not right at all. Lots of children hide in their closet, where no one can see or hear them. But, they need to talk, or else this can destroy their lives. Sometimes parents or people notice children behaving a certain way and we may not understand the reason why. It means they are suffering from unresolved issues and need to talk. Thank God for child psychology. Most parents who are looking for answers to their child's behavior, can now get the help they need.

In days gone by, so many people had a lack of knowledge. They were so naïve, that if a child complained to their parents that a man was making any kind of moves on them, some parents thought the child was just making it up, or probably had a nightmare, when in truth, and in fact, the child was serious. I have met and talked with people who have been sexually abused as a child, and now as an adult, it still affects them in different ways. Some have lost their self-esteem. I'm happy that more adults and children are now being able to talk about it.

We must be extremely careful who we bring into our lives and our home, especially when we have children. It is not every person you can trust. Some people are nothing but sickos. I believe that children need to be happy and have all rights to enjoy their childhood days, without someone taking advantage of them and ruining their innocence. Although we may not be able to be a bodyguard for our children to protect them from everything, if there is something that you could have done to protect your child, and you did not do it, trust me, like some of us, you will be on a guilt trip for the rest of your life.

Chapter 11

My Pity Party

Have you ever felt like you were in a pit and would never make it out, and wonder to yourself how you got there in the first place? You ask yourself, "Is this really happening? What did I do to deserve this?" Especially when every time you try lifting your head it is like something constantly beating it down.

There were times I felt I would never get out of the pit so instead, I decided to have a party in the pit. I called it my pity party. Satan joined in, invited his agents making a mockery of me. He was beating the drums and whispering in my ear that this is where you're going to stay, so you might as well give up, take a pill and chill.

He had me in his prey. This went on for years. I had a dream one night that I was visiting someone in a mental institution with a friend and her daughter, and while I was sitting in the waiting room, I opened my bag and found three bottles of pills. I was so confused, not knowing how they got there, so I looked at them, sulked and threw them back in the bag.

The bible says, *"Satan goes around like a roaring lion seeking whom he may devour."* (1Peter 5:8).

In that dream, I realized Satan had a plan. I was mentally drained, especially when I could not see a way out of my situation. I felt like there was no hope. And he was obviously planning to put me in an asylum. One of the things that bugged me the most is when I looked at the people who I had helped, and they in turn, treated me nastily, moving ahead while I sat in the ashes nursing those terrible wounds and sinking into the pit of depression. Some got married, and some were in a better position than me. To be quite honest, it was not that I was jealous of them, it was just that some people knew they had hurt me but showed no remorse. That bothered me for a while.

The enemy loves nothing more than to see a child of God unhappy. When I first read the story of Joseph, about how his brothers threw him in a pit, I couldn't control my emotions. I cried. I could not understand how his own brothers could have been so cruel to him.

It Could Be in Your Own Backyard

We do not have to ask if cruelty is an evil thing. And it's worse when it is being done by someone we trusted. Instead of removing this person from our life, we may have embraced them and found some excuse for their behaviour that would at least ease our pain and help us to feel better.

I came to realize sometimes we do not have to look very far when it is in our own backyard. And while they may not throw you into a literal pit, the hurtful things they do and say to you will sink you into a pit of depression. It makes it worse when you are looking for answers and they just brush you off like you are nothing and pretend they do not know what you are talking about. I'm sure some of you could identify with that. I can tell you it hurts. I am saying this because I've been there. In the bible it says that Joseph had to turn around and help his brothers who were so cruel to him.

I can't tell you how many times I've turned around to help people who hurt me repeatedly, until at one time I thought something was wrong with me. Instead of shunning them, I embraced them. Why? My answer to that is, I've come to realize that I must allow God to take control, understanding that he is bigger and greater than anyone and anything, including the pain that others inflicted on me. Sometimes God will prove a point by using you to help those that hurt you.

Matthew 5:44, *"Do good to them that hate you, and pray for them which despitefully use you and persecute you."*

That scripture is the test. How many people could show love to those that inflicted pain on them? Some people take pleasure in hurting others. When my husband was abusive to me, it didn't matter how much I cried, my tears never moved him one bit.

Although Jesus says we must forgive, it is not that easy to just say you forgive someone who treats your child as an outcast and physically and emotionally abuses them. We have the choice to forgive or to allow those people to keep hurting us. When I am angry and unhappy every day, this is not helping me or my children. Forgiveness does not mean the scar automatically disappears. Some wounds take a long time to heal, and at some time or other something reminds us of that horrid experience. I had to try and get my emotions under control. I'm going to use David in the bible as example. He was a man after God's own heart. We know that David was nothing close to perfect, he had his own flaws, and wasn't exempted from pain and disappointment. After being surrounded by enemies, he had to also deal with the betrayal, by his close friend, that brought him grief. Wow! I can't imagine the misery that he encountered. Let us take a look at what he had to say in Psalms 55:12-14 (NIV): *"If an enemy were insulting me, then I could of endure it; if a foe was rising against me, I could of hide. But it is you, a man like myself, my companion my close friend with whom I once enjoyed sweet fellowship with at the house of God, and walked around the worshipers."*

Some of us cannot believe the same people we loved and trusted have broken our hearts. Especially, when it comes from our own relatives that supposed to be the ones that we can trust and count on for support. Sometimes, the people some of us thought was our friend, turned out to be our worse enemy. When someone ruins our trust, it is hard to regain it. Sometimes the healing process is slow, but thank God, we don't have to hold onto the pain. As we give it over to Him, the burden gets lighter.

"And when you stand praying, if you hold anything against anyone, forgive them so that your father in heaven may forgive you your sins" (Mark 11:25).

Unforgiveness could hinder our prayer. Giving it over to God means you are not seeking revenge on the person, and instead you are allowing God to handle it for you.

There are some people who profess to be Christians and don't have a clue what the fruit of the Spirit means. Some are happy to blame the devil for their own evil doings. We all have a choice to do good or to do bad. When we disrespect someone that showed us nothing but love, we know it is an offence to our Creator, and in time he handles it. There are many reasons why a person who hurt you never apologize to you. One is because they willfully do it, two is because they know that sorry cannot undo the damage that is already done, another reason is pride.

The bible tells us pride comes before fall. Some people can be hostile, they never try to understand when you are hurting, and you don't want to become like them, so it is best to stay far away from such people.

Adjusting

When my children came to Canada they had to adjust. It was difficult for them, and whenever they needed help with schoolwork, I felt bad I could not help. It was different to how we did it in the Caribbean. I thought of taking some classes, so I could help them, but circumstances prevented me from pursuing that option.

I can't stop stressing on how difficult it is to feel the weight of guilt. It is not something that you can easily ignore when it is silently eating at you, especially where your children are concerned. If you show weakness as a parent, your children will look to someone else for guidance and will sometimes end up in the wrong hands. God has entrusted them in our care, and we must do our best. Sometimes we cannot do it by ourselves, and it is all right to ask for a little help when it's needed. To me parenting is like pastoring. This is why we have assistant pastors, to help out.

People look to their pastors for guidance, and if he comes across as being weak, then the congregation start complaining, and before you know it the numbers start decreasing. Some people look for other pastures to graze. It is the same way our children look to us for guidance and support.

When we are depressed it rubs of on our children and this can also affect their grades. So, at that time I try to do the best I can, by trying to make up for lost times. I have come to realize that we can never make up for time spent away from our children. However, in spite of everything, I thank the Lord that he was always watching over them, and that he has brought them safe to me.

There were times when they had their own struggles. With time, it was just amazing how they all did so well. They made it through high school and College, and graduated. I remember all the sleepless nights they had, when they were up studying for exams. I felt sorry for them. My son is good with computers, and he studied for almost four years to become a Computer Software Engineer. On the day of his graduation, hundreds of people of all different nationalities were there to witness the ceremony. It was heart touching for me, when I heard his name called and saw him walked across the stage with the other graduates. I was forever giving thanks to the Lord. I could see the joy and pride that he felt after all his hard work. My daughters, one hold a diploma in Counseling, and the other one in Child special needs Education. I'm proud of them for what they have accomplished by the grace of God. There are times when we need to adjust which is not always the easiest thing. It is just a part of life. Some people are afraid of changes, I'm one of them. Sometimes, only to find out that the very change we might be afraid of, is what we needed to get us on, or back on the right track. With determination we can achieve anything we want in life.

Chapter 12

Escaped Kidnap

Grenada is known as a safe island. People walk any time of the night without being afraid of anything. At the same time you never know what to expect. Like any place else in the world. We still need to be cautious. It was around 8 pm at night, and I decided to walk home after typing class, having no idea that I would get kidnapped. I was fourteen years old. A taxi pulled up alongside me, and the driver jumped out. He ordered me to get into the car, shouting at me that my uncle told him to give me a ride home. I knew it was a lie, for this man was known as the most dangerous man in the village where he lived, and most people were afraid of him. He opened the back door and pushed me into the car. At that point, I was traumatized. All I could feel was my heart racing.

I screamed at the top of my voice and pleaded with him to please let me out! He paid me no mind as he jumped into the driver's seat and drove off. Luckily, he had to slow down to turn the corner. That was my chance. Using all my strength, I pushed against the door and it swung open. I jumped out of the moving car and ran as fast as I could. I believe it must be the Lord that showed up that night, slowed down the traffic and caused me to escape from this man who intended evil toward me.

God will always make a way of escape.
—(1 Corinthians 10:13)

Chapter 13

Migration to Trinidad

In the early 1960s, I migrated to Trinidad to live with some relatives for a while. My mom accompanied me. I knew it was not the easiest decision for her, as my brother and sister were still young, and having to leave them was very difficult for her at that time. When the evening came for us to board the ship, my grandmother, my brother and sister were all there, and we were all seized by emotion, which saddened our hearts. People were busy getting on board. I remember there were old men on board playing the banjo, singing, "Now is the Hour," and just as we were about to board the ship we all hugged and cried.

It was a rough night on sea. The boat began to rock and rock; most people got nauseated and puked all over the place. I looked out the window. It was frightening. All I could see was blackness. As morning approached and darkness was fading, I began to feel better. It was the first time I would be meeting my great aunt and her husband. We were so excited to meet them when we came off the ship. They were both Christians, attending the Bethel Baptist Tabernacle Church at Kelly Kenny Street, Woodbrook. Every Sunday morning and evening we accompanied them to church. I gave my heart to Jesus in Sunday school and, after a brief time, got baptized.

Coming from a Catholic background, this new faith was so different. My mom also gave her heart to Jesus, got baptized and joined the choir. Every Sunday, the ladies in the choir dressed in white from head to toe and when they sang, they sounded like a choir of angels who had come down to Earth. Sitting in the pew, I could see my mom staring at me. No playing with my fingers or wiggling my toes. The look she gave me would say it all. I had to readjust my posture, like I was in a strait jacket.

My mom also got a job working in a guest house. She embraced the opportunity and decided to remain working there. It helped her to be in a better position to take care of us children.

Chapter 14

Returning to Grenada

I lived three years in Trinidad and then returned to Grenada, at the age of twelve, to continue my schooling. After a time, my great aunt wasn't nice to me. I could tell she didn't want me in her house, and I was unhappy being around her. With that, my mom and I went out looking for an apartment late one night, but we weren't successful, so, she asked someone from the church for me to spend a few days at their house. During those times I looked forward to returning to Grenada. I knew I would miss my mom, but it was a joy seeing my relatives at home again. Everything seemed so new to me. I reenrolled in my old School and felt like a princess. The students in my class especially the boys were all staring at me trying to get my attention, but I was just a shy twelve-year-old girl.

I remember this nice-looking tall handsome young man, he was somewhere between the age of sixteen to seventeen. He drew a picture of a girl and a boy hugging each other and gave it to me after school. I guess it was his way of telling me he liked me. The next morning, I gave it to the schoolmaster. Silly me. When the boy found out, he was afraid that he would get into trouble, and for that he skipped school.

I cannot believe I had done something so silly. A couple weeks after, I was standing at the bus stop with a box of groceries and this cute two seated car pulled up in front of me. To my great surprise, it was Lee, the same young man from my school stopped and offered me a ride home. After I got into the car, I felt like an idiot, knowing what I had done. Lee was a respectable young man and always cheerful. I thought he would be upset with me, but he never said a word about it. After he dropped me off to where I was going, I never laid eyes on him again.

In a conversation one day, his name came up, and I remember asking one of the girls about him, she said he went off to the Virgin Islands. This time I was a little more advanced in age, and for some reason I wasn't too happy when I heard that he was out of the country.

Chapter 15

The Teacher Asked Me Out on A Date

At the age of fourteen my teacher asked me out on a date. I thought he was completely out of place. "Why would a teacher ask his student on a date?" He felt I should not say no to him, so he was upset, and that day in class, I remember him whipping some of the students for their homework. He swung the whip across my back too, it stung like crazy, and was awful. I could not believe how cruel he could be.

At break time, some of the students would go down to the kitchen to get milk and cookies. He came into the kitchen and apologized, telling me he whipped me because he did not want the others to know he liked me. I did not think that made any sense, but I was too shy and feared he would be against me, so I didn't say anything. Back in those days, teachers would beat children with whips about thirty inches long. It was the cruelest thing, and some children carried scars from those whips.

The schoolmaster would put the boys across his desk and bench them with a piece of leather belt, twelve inches long and a quarter inch thick! It was brutal. Fear of getting the benching, would sometimes cause boys to skip school. The thought of it now, still makes me emotional. I had to walk many miles to school in the hot sun. At times my cousin and I could hear the bell ringing, signaling we were going to be late. We would run and make short cuts, jumping over ravines, to save our backs from the whip.

When my son was seven years old, he came home from school with a bruise on his hands, he told me he got beaten by his teacher. I can't believe the things some of us parents took so lightly and did nothing about it.

Chapter 16

Shock Cured His Asthma

I have repeatedly seen the hands of God, in every situation, good or bad, I have found myself in. My cousin Will and I decided to feast on some mangoes first thing one morning. Quite a few mangoes had fallen from the tree and we were quite excited—until something terrible happened that spoiled the fun. An electric wire was lying on the ground and neither of us had any idea it was live. My cousin picked it up and was instantly thrown to the ground. When I saw he had fallen and could not utter a word, I began to panic. I stood there watching him fight for his life. This went on for almost ten minutes. I was terrified, as fear threaded my mind, just hoping someone would come to his rescue.

I kept yelling, "Will! Will!" and talking to him. Then my uncle showed up! At that moment, I knew it was God who had sent him, just in time. My uncle was an electrician, so he knew what to do. He disconnected the wire from the house and, thank God, Will was set free. When he got up from the ground the palm of his hand was covered with small red and white blotches, and small cuts, which only took a few days to heal. There is a saying that out of evil cometh good. And, there was some good that came of that bad experience. Will used to suffer with asthma, and but after that incident, he was completely healed.

I realized it does not matter what we are going through, God already knows the great results that will come from a bad situation. Sometimes, when we are faced with difficult situations and cannot understand why, God is telling us he is still in control and he will make a way of escape for us. He will give us the victory, send help in time of trouble and also turn a horrible experience into a wonderful testimony, just as he did for my cousin Will, and for others. *God is never late.*

Chapter 17

Hit by Bus

Coming from school one evening, I was hit by a bus, while walking across a huge bridge, with a large river just at the bottom. Looking back at that incident is terrifying. If the bus had jammed me against that bridge, I would not have been here today. Thank God I'm here. It was a huge wooden bus, the kind where a woman would have to make sure she was not wearing tight clothes, or a mini skirt, as she would need to stretch her legs as high as possible to climb up into a seat. When the news of my accident reached my mom, she got there in no time. The driver drove me to the hospital for observation and I was released the very same day. All I had was a small bruise on my knee.

I remember the driver of the bus gave my mom forty dollars to buy ointment to put on my bruised knee, and out of that forty dollars, she also bought me a nice pair of gold slippers that I wore the same day, because I couldn't find one side of my shoe or something like that. And, that was all that came out of it. The most important thing is I'm alive, and I thank God his hands were upon me that day. Sometimes in life unpredictable things happen to us. We never know what lies ahead, which can be petrifying, and sometimes these things cause us to be more careful. After that, I avoided walking on that side of the road, I was much more cautious.

Chapter 18

The Guilt Trip

We all take a guilt trip at some time or another. When my two-year-old son got hit by a car, that is when my guilt trip began. That morning a young lady asked me to come with her to ask another woman, who lived in the neighborhood, to use her phone. I kept thinking if I had not gone to help her, my son would not have been hit by the vehicle. I remember my fiancé's brother was standing on the other side of the road, and he called out to my son.

My son, in his excitement, let go of my hand and ran across the road to meet him. A vehicle hit him, and he landed on the side of the road. I cannot explain how I felt at that moment. It was like my heart sank into my stomach. I was terrified. He ran to me and I picked him up in my arms, trembling, and we were both crying as I asked God to please help him. My fiancé's brother blamed me and told me it was my fault. Even though I knew it was, hearing it made me feel irresponsible.

I got into the car with my son and we headed to the hospital. They kept him overnight for observation. He was walking with a slight limp, which lasted for two days, but there were no bruises or broken bones. My child was all right. God had saved his life, and for that I am thankful. God is awesome!!! My son is now a grown man, but sometimes my mind reflects on that incident, and stirs up the guilt.

God is a God of Miracles

God works miracles every day. If we think about some of the things that he has saved us from we would be more appreciative and thankful.

Sometimes, dreams can be a warning, not to be taken lightly. I believe God gives us dreams, so we can pray against the dangers and plans of the enemy. The night before my son was hit by the car, I remember having a dream that we were walking that very same place and he let go of my hand and ran across the road. I cannot remember if I prayed about it, though. I was a Christian then, but not as dedicated as I am now. In many situations we face in our lives, we know it is the sustaining power of God that has kept us. There is a true saying that what does not kill you, makes you strong. Most of us can become crippled by some of the things life throws at us or even cause us to lose our minds. Thank God for his grace in time of need.

God Used My Son in The Saving of a Boy's Life

A few years ago, God used my son to help save the life of a little boy. The boy ran out in the traffic and left his mother standing in the yard where they lived. My son wasted no time. He ran after him, stopped the traffic and got the boy, while the mother stood there with her mouth opened and her hands clamped to her jaw, terrified and confused, bawling not knowing what to do in a horrific moment. I couldn't even imagine the thoughts that threaded this woman's mind. God sees everything before it happens, and he knew that he would use my son to help in saving a little boy's life in Canada.

I can say from my experience as a parent, watching our child hurt is the most difficult thing for any parent to experience. You could almost feel that heart wrenching pain. When my son got hit by a car, it was so terrifying. Only God knows the fear and the emotions that I encountered at that moment. Children feel the same for their parent. I remember back in 1980 when I got my leg fractured, my daughter who was only twelve years old looked at me with great pity in her little eyes. While I was at the hospital, she told me that one of the times she washed my night gown at home, all by herself. What a sweet way to show how much she loved and cared for her mommy. The most important things we can give to our children are LOVE and affection. Depriving a child of these two main elements can affect them for life. I love you. Some of us as children never really hear it. It doesn't mean that we don't love our children; we show it in action. As a baby we hear things like mommy, sugar plum, pumpkin, and so on. When my grandson was a baby he was so cute. I used to call him Cushi, not knowing what I was saying. It was just a cute little nickname that stayed for him. One day I decided to look up the word and to my surprise, it is a word that is used in the Hebrew Bible to refer to a dark-skinned person of African descent. I thought it was amazing to know this word actually had a meaning. Although it is not a common thing for parents in the Caribbean to always tell children they love them, I think it is something we should practice on a daily basis. It helps our children to feel much more secure.

Now she is all grown, and has children of her own. After all these years she said to me in a text, that mom, I wished at that time I could fix you. Oh, you wouldn't believe hearing her saying that was like something rose up from my stomach into my heart. I had to fight the emotions that I was feeling. And even now while I'm writing this, the feeling is revisiting me now in a stronger way. I never knew the pain that my little girl was feeling just watching her mother lying on the hospital bed with a fractured leg. It wasn't the easiest thing for her. I must admit for a child, especially that age, she had held it together well.

Chapter 19

The Hardest Decision

I left my children to come to Canada, and it was risky, especially not knowing the outcome. Leaving them with relatives, I was just hoping and trusting they would be all right. When I left for Canada, my son was eight and my two daughters were seventeen and four. My seventeen-year-old daughter was pregnant and already had responsibilities of her own. By the age of thirty-five, I was already a grandmother.

I remember, a few days before my flight, I wanted to change my mind. It was right around the time my aunt decided she would not be nice to me. I just could not understand why she was behaving so strangely with me, as soon as I told her my flight to Canada was confirmed.

My eldest daughter encouraged me, saying, "Mom, you shouldn't change your mind. This is to make a better life for all of us. You may have some challenges at first, but you will get through them and you will be all right." I must say that my daughter was right.

There are times when we are pushed to make decisions that cost us great pain. Even though that is all part of life, most of us seem to be stuck in the past and keep nursing those wounds. I realize that even though people may disappoint us, we are also at times disappointed in ourselves.

Chapter 20

Was It a Nightmare?

My son told me he fell from a crane in Grenada. It sounded unbelievable. I asked him, "What are you saying? Are you sure it was not a nightmare you had?" He was so calm talking about it, that I could not believe what I was hearing. For a moment I was seized. I just could not explain how I felt. I did not know how to react or what to say. I kept asking him, "Are you sure you didn't dream it?" I was trying hard to keep it together, as he was the kind of child who did not want to see his mother hurting or he would hurt, too. He said he knew it was the hand of God that caught him, and he had walked away without a scratch.

He said "Mom, that was proof that God is truly who he says he is, and he is in full control of my life." With what my son had been through as a child, and growing up, he knew that God was always watching over him, and that when no one else seemed to care, God does care.

I had many pity parties on my guilt trips. While still trying to be strong, I planted my trust in God, that he will give me strength from day to day. I know for sure that I cannot undo anything that went wrong. If I could, the first thing I would do is correct my mistakes, where I lacked as a mother. Most parents feel they have failed somewhere along the line. It can leave you with years of regret, which doesn't change anything.

"He giveth power to the faint, and to them that have no might,
He increases strength." (Isaiah 49:29)

Chapter 21

I Couldn't Believe I Failed

I remember when I was in primary school. I looked forward to the morning I had to write my common entrance examination to get into high school. I was positive I would do well and be showing off with my high school uniform just like other girls. Unfortunately, when the results came back, I cannot put into words how I felt. I was not only disappointed I had failed, I felt confused. I still do not understand why I failed. It could have been nervousness that had taken over. Although mathematics was never my favorite subject, spelling and reading were. I always scored nothing lower than ninety or one hundred. I never thought I was smart, especially after I failed a simple common entrance examination. I was so disappointed. And, with that, I dropped out of elementary school, and went to typing school.

At that time, I had given up on my dream of going to high school and felt that, somewhere along the line, I had been robbed. With the common entrance we still had to pay tuition to go to high school, and I do not know how it would have worked out. It would have put pressure on my mom, as she was not making much money.

My brother made it to college. He always scored at the top. He worked his way to earning a scholarship and went to one of the most recognized colleges on the island of Grenada, known as the Presentation Boys College. The uniform was a white shirt and white pants with a burgundy blazer. They looked amazing. After a couple of years, he took the General Certificate of Education examination and passed with flying colors. He then applied to Grenada Electricity Services, where he worked for a few months at the head office, before going on to work for Chase Manhattan Bank. From there, he quit and went on to Antigua to study hotel management. I guess it was quite an amazing adventure for him.

Chapter 22

Two Girls Want to Be Nurses

Marg and I had always wanted to become nurses when we grew up. As children we talked about it and pretended to be nurses. For the nurses' uniforms, we cut collars from old white shirts to make caps and used the back of the shirts to make aprons. We used to practice by helping out an old great aunt who had lived in the third last house on the hill from where we lived. The time had come when Marg had to leave for England to study nursing, and I knew I would miss her very much.

At that time, my uncle got me a job with a small printing company, known as the Torchlight. I was fourteen when I started working there. It was the easiest job, binding receipts books and putting them together. To me it was fun. I worked there for about three months and then got laid off. Soon after, I went to typing school, where I earned an elementary typing certificate. I also applied for a job at a clothing store for a couple of months, and then went on to work for McIntyre Brothers, Ltd. By that time, I was seventeen.

Someone told me they had a position for a typist, and since I typed forty words a minute I would qualify for the job. They gave me a position, but as a telephone operator, working on one of those ancient switchboards, where you had to turn the handle a few times to connect someone to a department. I can tell you one thing, having to turn that old switchboard handle for hours sure worked on my muscles, but having to deal with a mean boss was extremely difficult.

Whenever his line was buzzing, I would be apprehensive to take his call, as he was the kind of person who had no patience at all. The moment I would tell him all the lines were engaged, and that I would connect him as soon as a line became available, he would slam the receiver down, open his office door, yell at me at the top of his voice, and slam the door in my face.

There were times he would go as far as telling me to disconnect someone else's line and put his call through instead. I felt bad doing that, so at times I would first notify the people on the line and then connect him. On mornings when I had to go to work, I was nervous.

I was only making thirty-five dollars a week, and after one year I decided to leave the company and search for another job that would pay more. During my search I heard a new airline office was opening in Saint George's, and I applied there for a job. I got hired and was trained in ticketing and reservations. I loved my job, and every day I looked forward to going to work. I had the opportunity to meet people from all walks of life, and this time I was making two hundred dollars a month. That was a lot of money compared to what I had been making at my former job. When the airline decided to move out for whatever reason, I was disappointed.

Having earned a diploma in hairstyling and cosmetology, I thought being self-employed would be a good thing, so I began to search for a place and saw a space for rent in Saint George's. I shared it with a man who had a tailor shop, just next door. My rent was one hundred and fifty dollars a month. I had no money to start my business, so I asked my uncle to sign for me to get a small loan of five hundred dollars at the bank. My mom was in Trinidad working at the time. She sent me a few things I needed, which helped me to make a start. My friend, who also had a hairstyling salon, allowed me to borrow one of her hairdryers. It was quite a struggle, as I was not making enough money, and had to end up borrowing a hundred and fifty dollars to pay my first month's rent. It was unfortunate that everything went downhill after a horrible life experience. As you keep reading you will find out more.

Chapter 23

Bikini Contest

At the age of eighteen, I entered the Miss Bikini contest held at the Regal Cinema in Saint George's. Competing with other girls was a whole lot of fun. Hundreds of people swarmed the place that night and I was excited. I was just looking forward to sporting my leopard print swimsuit. I could feel my legs jiggling as nervousness took over. I remember walking three quarters of the stage, but then quickly running off and dashing back to the dressing room when I noticed all the men eyes were on me.

At the end of the contest the winners were announced, and I heard my name called for first runner up. I was thrilled. The day after, I ran into a couple of people who were at the show. They all congratulated me and asked me why I ran off the stage. They had been confident I would leave there with the Miss Bikini crown. In the first place, I wondered where I got the nerve to enter a bikini contest. Being shy is something I had to deal with from the time I was a child, and this contest somehow helped increase my confidence.

Chapter 24

Trinidad

Who Are These Men in Black?

I went back to Trinidad in my mid-teens, and I got a part-time job working at a small electrical appliance store to make a little pocket change. I would always walk through Independence Square, after I finished work, as it was a shortcut to get to a taxi. That evening, three men, dressed in black suits and holding briefcases, were sitting on a bench, looking quite suspicious. In my mind, I asked, why are they staring at me. I tried walking another way, but they were determined and walked towards me saying, "What we want to say to you is very urgent and very important."

I was alarmed just hearing those words, and as they continued, I became more apprehensive. Next, they said, "Someone is trying to do something bad to you and we will help you, but you will have to give us some money. If you do not allow us to help you, death will be your destiny." They asked me how much money I had on me. I told them I only had five dollars to pay the taxi.

"When do you get paid?" they asked. I was honest and told them I got paid on Friday. They said you would wait for me right there. That left me confused. I did not know of any other way to get to the taxi stand, so I had to take the same route all the time. Friday came and they were at the very same spot waiting. They approached me again, and while talking to me they were writing something in a notebook. I could not tell what they were writing. I reached into my purse, took out my thirty dollars, and handed it over to them and started crying. It was the hardest thing to do. When I got home I told my mom, and from the time I started telling her what happened, she knew those men were up to no good. She quoted Psalm 27:1 "The lord is my light and my salvation whom shall I fear."

My mom was a strong Christian and firmly believed in the word of God, and that nothing could harm you once you trusted in God. Thank God for a mother who spent time on her knees for her children. Otherwise, I do not know how I would have made it. We are living in a world with a whole lot of evil. Satan has no conscience, and anyone that allows him to use them as his agent, has no conscience themselves.

We must always stay under God's protection. The devil can only go so far, as God allows him.

He that dwells in in the secret place of the most high, shall abide under the shadow of the Almighty. (Psalms 91)

CHAPTER 25

Grenada: A Day of Horror

It was June 19, 1980, a day that went down in history, and the day I became aware of who God really is in a time of trouble. I closed my salon for the evening, and then I and the young lady working with me decided to take a walk to Queens Park Savannah, to witness the grand parade. While I never knew what was awaiting me, God already knew it was a day I would never forget, and a day that would go down in history. When we got to the park, the pavilion and ground were packed with people. It was a day mixed with sunshine and rain, which turn into a day of horror and pain. Yes, horror and pain.

I joined the others at the back of the pavilion. We were all excited about the parade and looked on in admiration. As soon as it was over, Prime Minister Maurice Bishop went on stage to give his speech. While everyone was listening to his message, something terrible happened. We heard an explosion, and someone yelled out, "A bomb!"

That is when my mind flooded with thoughts and it felt like butterflies flying around my stomach. Yes, it was terrifying! The crowd scattered, and people were running in different directions, scampering for their lives. I was one of them. I was amazed that some people were smart enough to stand still, and these were the people who did not get hurt. A whole lot of us were running down the steps, falling over each other; some got their bodies trapped and some got their feet trapped between the stairs. The only parts of my body I could move were my two hands. I held them up in the air, crying, "Lord, help me! Lord, help me!!!"

My mind was going crazy with frightening thoughts. "What if I don't survive? What will happen to my children? Who will take care of my son?" My two-year-old son I had left with my grandmother, and my ten-year-old daughter were living with her grandmother. In my distress, in that terrifying moment, I caught the attention of a young man. I remember he was wearing a burgundy shirt. He was one of the ones helping pull people out from the stampede, and he came to my rescue. I then realized I couldn't move my right leg. It was an indication that something was wrong. I could hear some of the people saying her leg is broken. Immediately, one of the ladies who worked with the government drove me to the hospital.

The doctors and nurses were extremely busy that day. The announcement went out there was over ninety injured people, including doctors and nurses. When I arrived at the hospital, the doctors immediately put me under anesthetic. I had a vision where I saw myself walking in front of my salon, in the same clothes I wore that very day. I guessed it was a flashback, reminding me that life must not be taken for granted. Waking up from the anesthetic, I could hear my cousin, who had just graduated from one of the universities in England. She was also the matron of the hospital where I was admitted. I could hear her calling my name, saying, "Barbara, it's Elsa!"

When I woke up, one of the nurses told me I was preaching and asking the Lord to heal me from the crown of my head to the soles of my feet. I always knew how to talk to Jesus, especially in times of trouble. I knew I needed him there with me just to feel his loving arms around me, and to let me know everything would be all right. I could see a piece of metal in my right leg, shooting out from one side to the other. The doctor explained to me the reason for the metal was that I had suffered a compound fracture. My leg needed to remain in traction for a few weeks, so it would heal properly. They moved me from one room to the next. As I glanced across to the other side of the room, I saw another young woman, who had also suffered a broken leg from the stampede. Another young girl lost one of her legs and lost her sister in the explosion.

My mom was in Trinidad when she got the news. It took her no time to get on the plane. When she arrived at the hospital, I could see the look of sadness on her face, and that she was still trying to hold it together. The pain of seeing her daughter lying in a hospital bed with a fractured leg, could not have been easy. She prayed for me night and day and gave me words of encouragement. My daughter told me when my mom was at home she would not eat. She cried all the time. But, when she came to visit me she would not allow me to see she was hurting.

Chapter 26

Cuban Bone Specialists Disappointed

The Cuban bone specialists taking care of me said there was no need for surgery on my leg because I was young, and it would heal fast. In two to three months, I would be walking again. Unfortunately, the specialists were leaving for vacation in a couple of days, so the hospital's head doctor took charge. I was distraught when he said he would need to do surgery on my leg. To me, he was just waiting for the bone specialists to leave, so he could take over. I tried to talk him out of it, but he was determined, and this caused me more distress.

My mom pleaded with him, expecting he would change his mind, but it was his word against ours. The next morning came and they wheeled me into the operating room to perform the surgery. I cried my heart out. After I recovered from the anesthetic, nothing I ate would stay down. My mom was very worried, and she prayed and asked the Lord to help me. It took quite a few minutes before my stomach settled and felt better.

My mother had taken time off from her job in Trinidad, and due to that, she could not extend her stay any longer. She had to leave in a matter of days. The young lady who used to work with me in my salon came to look in on me the day she was leaving. I heard her asking the young lady, to please take care of me and started crying. It was sad to see her in such an emotional state.

When the Cuban doctors returned, I could see that they were quite disappointed! They looked at the chart hanging in front of my bed, and they were talking and looking at each other and shaking their heads. With the look on their faces, I could tell they were not happy that the other doctor had performed surgery on my leg. I was not the happiest person either, but it was already done. Come to think of it, that doctor should not have gotten away with something like that. He should have been sued! But in the Caribbean, nobody thought about suing anybody. I had never heard of anyone doing that until I came to Canada.

I remained in the hospital for one month, and during that time my dad only came to see me one time. I could tell he was upset. His eyes told it all. His words to me that he was planting corn, while I was at the rally, made me feel worse. Lies were going around that I was thinking of committing suicide. The thought of suicide never crossed my mind for one second.

I also learned something from that painful experience. I learned that the people I thought I could rely on were not there for me. I had one good friend who I used to spend weekends with, at her house, before the incident. After I came out of the hospital she came and looked in on me after work and spent a couple of hours with me, which I appreciated very much. Then, I went back to my lonely room.

She promised she would come back the following day, and when she did not show up, the pity party continued. I remember calling her and crying on the phone like a baby. I kept saying to her you promised to come back and look in on me but did not. I felt no one cared about me. Well, that did not make her feel good at all. I could tell she was not happy with what I was saying, and she then explained the reason she could not come by. I allowed my emotions to get the better part of me, and for that I felt silly.

We can become emotionally distraught when something painful happen to us. We begin to think and feel that no one cares about us. It takes a lot of courage to remain positive and stable minded during pain and disappointments. I knew I had to trust God, that he would see me through this difficult period in my life. And though many people predicted the worst and some did not have my best interests in mind. I had to remain positive, picture myself walking without those crutches and having a beauty salon again. I had to believe that something good would come out of a bad situation. The apostle Paul encourages us in Philippians 4:8 *"Fix your thoughts on things that are true, honorable, right, pure lovely and amiable."*

That is exactly what I did.

Chapter 27

Jealousy Rejoices Hope Wins

I ask myself the question, why is it some people rejoice when others get hurt? There were so many jealous and upsetting remarks that were cast after my leg was fractured. I said, Jealous remarks, because I could not believe the awful things that I was hearing. Just imagine you're lying on a hospital bed with a fractured leg and hearing people on the outside saying you are not attractive because you have a broken leg, you are thinking of committing suicide and you would not be able to step in heels again. How would you feel? Doesn't that sound like jealousy talking? I can't imagine how people think. It baffles me. After that incident at the park, I've learned so many things. I learned that there were people who smiled with me, but they weren't genuine. I think we must be careful how we treat others, especially when they are in a vulnerable state.

It was a time when I felt isolated and lonely. This has brought me to a closer relationship with Jesus Christ, knowing he will never leave me nor forsake me. We all live in a world where people can be very cold and uncompassionate. It may affect us, but we should not allow them to change us from whom God expects us to be.

(Romans 12:21) *"Be not overcome of evil but overcome evil with good."*

I knew despite everything that was happening to me, God had a great plan for my life. I wasn't going to allow anyone, nor anything to destroy my faith and trust.

There are those that will wish you well, and then there are those that would not wish you well. I understand that is not everyone that would like me. At the same time, some people don't even have to have a reason to not like you. I also learned it doesn't matter what you do for people, if they don't like you, they would not want anything good for you. Jealousy and envy are the two things that cause people to go crazy at times. No one knows how I was struggling when I opened my salon, but when they passed by and saw my name up, they cast ugly remarks.

The minute you try to make a step up in life, some people will do all in their power to throw things at you to knock you down. You must stand strong and keep going. (Romans 8:31) *"What then shall we say in response to these things? If God is for us, who can be against us?"*

There are those who may have rejoiced after the incident, but that didn't change who I am, I still talk with them. I realize those people are not happy with themselves and they need a change of heart. When others rejoice at your pain it is not a good feeling. Knowing Jesus went through more than that for us, we should be of good courage. There are also people who professed to be Christians and show no compassion. Therefore, we shouldn't waste time worrying over people who have no sense of direction in their life. Thank God, bless them and leave the rest to Him and keep moving forward. Those are the same people that will come and ask you for help one day. I have seen it time and time again.

I have come to the point, where I have no time to feel bad about any unpleasant remarks that have been cast against me anymore. I'm too busy trying to work out my own Salvation.

The Bible says that *we must work out our own Salvation with fear and trembling.* (See Philippians 2:12-13.)

Not one of us can work out someone else's Salvation for them. My sister and I used to think that we could live on our mother's Salvation. After a time, we both came to realize that is not so at all. Each one of us must be responsible and give account to the creator for our life and the way we live on this earth. Our hope is in Christ, and if we keep that hope alive, it would not disappoint us. We are on the winning side.

See Romans 5:5 "And *hope does not put us to shame."* (NIV).

Chapter 28

My Malnourished Son

When I came out of the hospital and saw my son, my heart was broken. I could see my poor child was suffering from malnutrition. His little tummy was like a balloon and his eyes looked so weak. It tore my heart. But despite that, I looked at the good side of things. Again, I thank God for watching over him, that he has kept him safe, and we are all in the land of the living.

If I were to write a book of thanks to the Lord, one book would not be able to contain it, as I have so much to give Him thanks for. When the storm is raging, we should never forget who is in the midst. It may not look like he is there at the time, but he carries us through. When we survive the storm, we may come out with a few bruises and broken bones, and sometimes we may come out with a limp, but Jesus is our healer and we are here to tell the story. I remember Pastor Raymond Cyrus said these words, "It doesn't matter if you are walking with a limp and God call you to preach, you will preach." Some of us are preaching but still walk with an emotional limp. As we commit ourselves to God and his word, he will build us up." (See Acts 20:32)

Sometimes God uses a situation to get his children back in line. We never realize our mistake until something painful happens and we know that it is God that is trying to get our attention. We may think that everything that happen to us is the devil, but most of the times we are wrong.

Chapter 29

How I Met My Husband

A few weeks after I was out of the hospital, I was spending a couple of days at the guest house where I used to have lunch when I was working with the airline. One day, an attractive young man came to visit the lady who owned the guest house, and I noticed that he was staring at me. I can tell it was admiration, mixed with pity.

Later, I found out from the lady that the he was interested in me and would like to get to know me. He invited the lady and me to his birthday party which was the following day. I was somewhat flattered as I did not think anyone would be attracted to a woman on crutches.

He had just turned twenty-nine. It was just three people present at the party. The lady who owned the guest house cooked, and we ate and enjoyed ourselves. When he asked me to go swimming with him, I looked at him and said, "You must be crazy. I am not going swimming with this scar on my leg." He would not take no for an answer. I thought, since he insists, it might be a good idea for me to follow him down to the beach. I knew I couldn't swim but at least the salt water would help to strengthen my leg. He held my hand, and we both walked to the beach.

We ran into a couple that we knew, and when they asked me how my leg was coming along, he answered that I was shy and worried about the scar on my leg. I remember one of them gave me a look and said, "What is wrong with you girl? Give God thanks that you can walk instead of worrying about the scar on your leg."

At that time, it was like a light bulb turned on, and I realized how much I did have to be grateful for, instead of worrying about a scar on my leg. But, this never erased the fact that I was disappointed the doctor did surgery on my leg. If he had left it in traction, as the bone specialists recommended, I would not have ended up with a useless and embarrassing scar on my leg.

My friend came up with the idea that the sea water would help to strengthen my leg, and that I should live close to the beach. He offered to rent me his basement. I took him up on the offer, and we both used to go swimming twice a day, at four o'clock in the morning and at six o'clock in the evening. By the kindness and the interest he showed me, I knew he liked me. In a short space of time, we started dating, and during that time I observed that whenever he had a drink he would act differently. That scared me, but still, within a year we planned to get married. I went off on a vacation to Trinidad for a couple weeks, by that time I was struggling with the feelings of whether I wanted to get married or not. I remember calling him on the phone and telling him I needed more time, I'm not sure if I really wanted to get married. He sounded nervous on the phone and told me we already set a date, so let's go ahead with it.

The night of the wedding he had a couple drinks. I was so embarrassed when he started yelling at my four-year-old son for touching his watch he had left on the table. My dad was at the wedding. I remember asking him that night if he was happy now that I was married. He whispered that he was not happy because I had not yet met my husband. Parents always sense when something is wrong. After the reception, my husband, my son and I went back to the house where we resided, and for days he talked about the watch. There was no reason for him to keep talking about it. The child did not do anything to the watch, it worked perfectly fine. That is when I realized I would be in for a whole lot of problems with this man.

Chapter 30

Ignoring the Signs

So many times, we ignore the signs and fall into a trap that we could have avoided.

All the signs were there before I got married, but love is a strong thing, and the bible says it covers a multitude of faults. God also uses signs to show us what we should avoid, but we never take note. Before I got married I remember saying to a neighbor who knew this man very well, that I will pray for him to change, but when he changes, I don't want him to marry any other woman but me. I'm not sure if that makes sense. Here again no one else is to be blame but me. If we only obey when the Lord is speaking to us, it will save us from all the unnecessary mistakes and the problems that we brought on ourselves. There is always a lesson to learn, and sometimes we learn the hard way. I was still in the hopes that he would change his ways. I remember him telling me that as soon as we had a child he would change. Somehow, I had believed him. But as time went by, things got worse. Our daughter was born in 1984, and while I was pregnant, I remember him knocking my head on the floor one evening when he came home drunk. It was a rough five years in my marriage.

Every Friday evening as a rule, he would start drinking. It was the only time he would notice my son and pretend he was playing with him, which was weird. When he was sober, he was cruel and mean to him. A couple of times I took his bottle of vodka and emptied it down the sink. I was so fed up with all the abuse that, one day,

I decided to pour some vodka in a glass and drink it to see how it feels to be drunk, and go to bed and sleep off my worries, or maybe we could both get even with each other, and he would like that. My mouth was on fire, but I did not get drunk.

It was the first and last time. I don't understand why people put themselves through this torture.

At times, when he got drunk and vomited up the place, I was the one who cleaned it up. It took a lot out of me and I wanted to vomit myself. I was always an independent person and never depended on him for anything. I owned a small hair salon and worked outside the home to take care of my children. It was my second hair salon after the one I had before the incident. Even though I was not making a lot of money from my business, it was still helpful to me in some ways. There were times he would come home from work drunk and he would throw knives at my feet. The knives would get stuck in the wood flooring just about half an inch from my feet. He came home from work one evening and my son was having dinner, he slapped him and emptied his dinner outside the window and sent him to bed crying. It broke my heart. He would not allow my child to sit next to me, not even when he was hurting and needed my comfort. My son was so afraid of him, that he became so nervous whenever he was around. There were times when he slapped him so hard, that he peed on himself. He was a four-year-old innocent child. I cannot understand why my husband was so cruel to him.

There were times when I was cooking, he would run me out of the house. I would go to a relative's house or to the house of another Christian lady who lived closed by, just to clear my mind. When I returned, he would have already eaten all the food, leaving none for me. One day while nursing my daughter, he came to pick a fight with me. I ran outside the house and he came after me, and he pulled her away from my breast and told me to go my way and leave his child for him. She was only two weeks old. He threw the lit candle and saucer at me while putting my son to bed. He took the baby away from me and threw her on the bed, she knocked her forehead against the wall. Until today my daughter still has a tiny scar close to her eyebrows. I thank God it wasn't her eyes. One Sunday evening my husband sharpened a cutlass and sat in the living room with it across his leg, telling me I was not going to see the next day. He put the cutlass to my neck and the point of it brushed my neck. There was a bit of blood, not anything too serious, but it could have been worse. I jumped through the back door and headed for the police station. Just imagine, my three-year-old had to witness something like that. After I made the report to the police, they took him to a Mental Institution for a few days and said the alcohol was getting to his head. I decided to pack up my clothes and leave for a while, hoping that when they released him he would change. On top of all that, I still went to visit him, and brought him food. He was catholic, and I used to attend the Pentecostal Church. There were times he would get to the church I attended before me, promising me he would change, but it was the same thing over and over.

At this point, it was crucial for me to decide for the children's safety and for myself. After being in the marriage for five years, I realized that we had a bad relationship, which was lacking love and compassion from his end. First communication was a barrier, then the respect and trust were no longer there. It was a total mess, and to me all my efforts were in vain. It became clear to me that I had no joy and many people saw it on my continence. On top of all that, I understand that he was cheating, and when I confronted him about it, he did not deny it. Yet, I still thought that if he is willing to change, I would forgive him and give him another chance. I told him on many occasions if he did not change his behavior, we would have to go our separate ways. However, that still did not bring him to a realization that he needed to change, so I went to relatives for two weeks just to get away and clear my head, but he came and persuaded me to come back. At that point, he was apologetic and promised me that he would change for good and never treat me the way he treated me in the past ever again. And since I had loved him, I decided to take another chance at it, because I really wanted our marriage to work. However, I finally realized that he was never going to change, and he did not want to get any help that was offered to him. After a time, we moved to my grandparents' house in the countryside where I grew up.

One Friday night he came home drunk waking me from my sleep with punches at the back of my neck. This time, I decided I'm not going to put up with this any longer, so I took his small suitcase and threw it over the balcony. I know he wasn't expecting I would do that, he looked at me and he said something valuable belonging to you would pay for it. When I went back into the bedroom, I couldn't believe he took a knife and slashed my favorite church dress that was hanging next to my window. That was a serious indication that I was in serious trouble with this man. I said Lord you need to do something, or else I will do something. There was a time I suggested we take a trip to Trinidad for a vacation, and it seemed like he was all for it, but as soon as he drank, he asked me if I wanted to take him to Trinidad to get rid of him. He was a very stubborn man. I remember one day he was drunk, and he was saying that his father was abusive to his mother, so he was getting revenge for that. At this point, I realized that I was dealing with someone who had a lot of deep-seated issues, that I could not help him with no matter how much I wanted to or even tried. For this reason, I knew I needed to get out from this abusive relationship as soon as possible. I realized I needed love, appreciation, and respect among other things. I could not allow myself and my children to continue living in that situation, and I knew I had to get out of it for us to have a better life. I needed some balance and to also invest in myself, so I could stay healthy spiritually, mentally and physically to take care of my children.

I do not think it is God's will for a person to sit down in an abusive relationship. When love and respect is thrown out the window, look for the door. If someone loves you, they would not keep hurting you. If a person stays in a relationship for the children's sake, that is not a good excuse. If a person thinks such behavior is acceptable, then they need help. Children should not have to witness such things. It's important that we teach our children good morals and values. We set good standards for them, and try to do our best as a good parent would, but we never think how unhealthy it is for our children to live in an unhealthy home, having to watch their parent fighting and not getting along with each other. This can have a psychological effect on them. We cannot change a person, but we can change the way we think. And we must do what is best for ourselves and our children. Too many times I have heard women say they only remain in the marriage because of the children.

That is a lame excuse. We need to come up with a reason much stronger that. Sometimes it is for our own selfish reasons. You love them so much, that you just can't see yourself without them. And with that we can't even think straight. We disregard our children's feelings and put ours first. We prefer to stay and take the abuse. I know of a couple that used to fight regularly, and when you asked them why they fight so much their answer was because they love each other. That is the silliest thing I've ever heard. Some women think if their man doesn't hit them, he doesn't love them. I've learned from older people, that, if a man slaps you the first time, and you don't put a stop to it, it is likely he will do it again. Unfortunately I never experienced true love in my relationship. I thank God instead of being bitter, I can now empathize with those that are unfortunately experiencing the same problems, and use my experience to help them.

When my daughter asked me why I stayed with her dad, knowing he was abusive, all I could say to her was, that I was hoping he would change. I knew it was unhealthy for me to remain in an abusive marriage. But I managed to get out of it. It did not matter how much I loved him, after a time I became apprehensive and I just did not want to see him. I knew it was time for us to go our separate ways. If something doesn't fit, then we shouldn't force it for many reasons. One of the reasons is, it complicates things, it is dangerous, and we would not be happy.

The sad thing is, unfortunately some people stayed in an abusive relationship that cost them their life.

Chapter 31

Waiting Was Hard

Having to wait many months to get my Canadian work permit was not easy. I had a part-time babysitting job, just nine hours a week, so I could send some money and clothes back home to my children. I had to travel over two hours to work, by train and bus. When I got home, my back would be sore from sitting on those long rides. I thought it was best for me to keep searching, so I applied for a job at a fast food restaurant, just walking distance from where I lived.

It was still difficult for me, as the moment I noticed someone coming to the counter with a badge on their shoulder, I would be apprehensive, thinking it was an immigration officer. I stayed on the job for two weeks before telling the manager I could not work under those conditions. One day, I picked up the newspaper, and as I flipped the pages what caught my eye was that a spiritual healer wanted someone to work as a housekeeper. Without hesitation, I picked up the phone and called. I said, "Sir, I'm just answering your ad. I'm interested." He told me to come for an interview. I asked him if he believed in spiritual healing and he said, "Yes." I asked him if he believed in praying for the sick to heal them, and he said, "Yes."

Somehow, when I got off the phone with him something was troubling my spirit. I decided to walk with my bible to the interview. When I arrived at his doorstep, I saw Psalm 23, written on the door. My spirit was still troubled. I rang the doorbell and a well-dressed gentleman came to the door and invited me in. He asked me to have a seat and said he would be back in a few minutes. He was the owner of the house, the same person I spoke with on the phone.

Those few minutes gave me the chance to talk with God and ask him to guide me. I opened my bible. My eyes fell on a scripture reading about the water and the lies and be careful that evil come upon thee. At that moment, I knew God was warning me against the evil that was going on in that place. Since then, I never laid eyes on that scripture again. God talks to his children through his word, through the Holy Spirit and through others. All we must do is listen attentively. I wanted to change my mind, so I called someone I knew very well and told them about it, and what the Lord had shown me. This good friend, with a good heart, saw my difficulty in finding a job, especially as I had just come to Canada and had my children back home to care for. I thought ok, I will give it a try.

The owner of the house asked me to follow him downstairs, and I saw a table with over ninety glasses of water filled to the top without spilling. I had never seen anything like that before. My eyes beheld all kind of things that described evil. But, I needed to work and get money to send to my children. Not having a work permit, it was difficult finding jobs. He was obviously aware of that. I remember him saying to me, you are a nice brown-skinned girl, and one day I will have my way with you.

I did not believe him. I thought he was joking until one day when his girlfriend went out and he came upstairs laid on the couch and asked me to make him a cup of tea. He then pulled me to him, and before you know it, this robust man start wrestling me down to the couch, trying to have his way with me. It did not matter how much I tried pushing him off he would not stop. A car pulled up in the driveway, it was his girlfriend. I blamed myself for not taking heed to the warning God had given me from his word. I remember when I told a friend about it, he was quite upset and said too many women have been taken advantage of when they don't have their work permits.

After what had happened that day, I felt uncomfortable on the job, so I decided to quit and look for work elsewhere. After a couple weeks, I checked out an agency who took care of the elderly and I got hired. I was assigned to a client with Alzheimer's disease and it was quite difficult to work with her. She thought I came to take over her house. I wasn't allowed to do anything in the house. She pointed a kitchen knife at me saying, "You better be a good girl now, or else." At that point, I became apprehensive.

That day, she was so upset, that she left the house in a rage, jumped into her car and drove off. I was confused. I couldn't understand how a person with Alzheimer's could be driving. The husband said when she was upset, she would drive to her daughter's house which is not far from where they lived. That put my mind at ease. After she came back, she was in a better mood. She asked me to help her in preparing dinner. Surprisingly, she invited me to the table to have dinner with her and her husband. The next day, I went to work, it was the same problem. This time I called up the agency and let them know what was happening.

The husband wasn't happy that I was leaving. He said he needed the help and that his wife couldn't help the way that she was behaving. I already knew it would be impossible for me to continue working under those conditions, and nothing could have made me change my mind. I was never trained to work with people that suffer with Alzheimer's disease. I had no idea what I was getting into. I love taking care of the elderly, and some of them are quite interesting. But I realize Alzheimer's is a terrible disease, and in order to work with those that have it, a person must be well educated and trained.

Chapter 32

Immigration

I had to get out of bed at four o'clock in the morning to make the long trip by bus and train, to the immigration office downtown Toronto. I felt so weak and nauseated when I arrived at the office from the long drive. People were already lined up outside. I had gotten there early, yet I saw people who came after me left before me. I wondered why. I remember pulling up a couple of chairs and lying down, because I was feeling so sick.

An immigration officer looked over at me from behind her desk, asking me if I was tired. At that point I burst into tears, and said, "Yes, I am so tired." I was the last person to leave the immigration office that day. Well, months rolled on before I could finally get my work permit, but when I got it I felt free like a bird. I was able to work without having to look over my shoulder. I sent for my children, one by one. It was a long wait, but it was a happy reunion. I then had to wait for my permanent resident card. It seemed like it took forever.

We had to cross the border to take care of some documents and come back in. We took the bus and train, and stayed in a hotel for the night, and I was quite happy to know my children and I were now landed immigrants. It was like a load lifted off me. I had waited seven years before I could finally board a plane to go back to my homeland and visit.

Chapter 33

Question by My Five-Year-Old

The first question my five-year-old daughter asked me when she came to Canada was, "Why did you leave me? Why didn't you take me with you to Canada?" Well, of course, that is a valid question for any child to ask their parent. It was quite difficult trying to explain the reason to her, as she only saw it from a child's point of view. She told me she felt like she was on her own, like no one cared.

When my son came from Grenada I noticed a scar on his hand. No one had ever written to tell me that my child had an accident. When I asked him what had happened, he said he and my nephew were playing downstairs in the house one day, and he got cut on glass from a broken window.

He had to get stitches, and the person who went to the medical station with him was my nephew, who is only about six months older than my son. Imagine two small children walking all the way down to the medical station all by themselves with blood pumping out of my son's hand. He said to me, "Mom, I could have fainted." Well, I thank God he didn't. He said people were asking, "Child, where is your mother?" He told them his mother was in Canada. Again, my heart cried tears, wishing I had been there for him.

He said many times he wondered what was wrong with him, that it seemed like no one liked him. And there were times he felt alone and neglected. He had a little dog that he used to play with, but it got killed and he was so sad. But, when my uncle came to visit, he would run after the car, as he would be sad that my uncle was leaving. He said one day, the car wheel ran over his feet. It happened so fast, he did not even have time to feel it. There was no phone in the family house, so there were times I would call the neighbor to speak with my children. I wanted to hear their voice and to know that they were all doing fine, but I remember a lady said to me, please make haste and send for your son. They are not treating him good at all. Imagine, as a mother hearing these things and you are thousands of miles away.

I knew I had to hurry up and get things going. I remember there was a lady that came to Canada, shortly after I sent for my children, and I can recall, when she saw my son, she said to him, "You are the same respectable little boy. Even though they did not treat you well, you haven't changed." When my four-year-old daughter told me she got hit by a car and no one knew about it, I thought that she had a dream or a nightmare. I knew nothing about that. It seems like a lot was hidden from me. There's a saying what you don't know won't hurt you. Sometimes what you don't know can still hurt you.

There are many people carrying around physical scars even from their childhood days, but that unseen scar could be a silent destroyer. As my daughter would say the physical leads to the emotional, and it affects you in many ways. There are times when she would still talk about the bad experiences that she had after I left for Canada. She told me she was forced to grow up in a mature environment. She said that her story is one of an adult. I don't know what to say to her. There is nothing I could say to her, that will make her feel better. It is the worst feeling hearing your children saying to you, it is too late now. Even though you know it is the truth, you still feel terrible. I can't begin to tell you the sadness I felt in my heart, just hearing those words. I must allow her to have her moment. This means she is still in the healing process. Keeping in mind that my children are my responsibility, I should have planned better for them. I don't need anyone to tell me that.

It wasn't a mistake that I came to Canada, but it was a mistake that I didn't plan properly for my children. My son told me that one year, felt like five years. Sometimes we find ourselves doing the right thing the wrong way, that brings us pain and regrets. There are times they all would say to me, "Mom thanks for bringing me up to Canada." Hearing those words from them and how grateful they are, makes me feel good. At least something good came out of a messy situation. I could choose to sit and beat up on myself all day long, but it wouldn't make a difference. The only thing I must learn to change is my mindset.

Changing my mindset helps me to see things from a different perspective. I know that I cannot undo what is already done. And, yes there are times when I think of it my emotions rise. And when my son said to me, "Mom instead of focusing on the bad that already happened, let us thank God that the worst didn't happen." Hearing these words, many times have helped me to keep my emotions under control.

Chapter 34

Reaching Out for Help

Some people may think asking for help shows weakness, and they struggle with their feelings until it's too late.

No man is an island. There are things we cannot deal with on our own, and at some point, we need the help of others.

After years of sweeping things under the carpet, there comes a time when it all catches up with you. This has been quite an emotional experience for me.

The pain was so intense, after hearing from others how my son had been ill-treated in my absence. I realized I needed help, so I called the 700 Club, Christian Broadcasting Network, to have someone pray for me. I could imagine what my mom felt when I was abused by my husband and would run out of the house late at night to find a phone to call her in Canada. I would tell her about the latest episode, and she would pray for me over the phone. So, when I called the 700 Club, a woman came on the line and I began to pour my heart out, telling her I was hurting over some unresolved issues and that I needed some prayer.

Imagine: A couple years passed before I could ever let this terrible feeling out. And that is the mistake I made. At least I should have let these people know what they did was wrong. But, instead I behaved like I didn't know anything. Sometimes, I wonder if something is wrong with me. I never treated any one of them differently; I loved them the same. I swept things under the carpet, wept in silence—until one day when I heard it from another relative. This time, I couldn't pretend any longer.

I thought I would feel better after the lady on the prayer line finished praying. I could not believe it, but the pain elevated, and I felt like my heart was tearing. It felt so weak, like it was ready to collapse. It was the most frightening experience, and I needed to get this off my chest. I was afraid if I didn't, I might have ended up in a hospital bed.

I was prepared for the reaction I would get already knowing who I was dealing with. When I was leaving for Canada, that person was not the happiest and did not wish me well. I remember her accusing me of having an affair with her husband when I was a young teenage girl. I couldn't believe what I was hearing. I remember telling the husband about it, and he asked which possible time was that? He himself was surprised. I could not believe that she would ever accuse me of something like that. It blistered my heart. After so many years, it still bothers me. I often wonder if that was the reason she treated my child the way she did. I know people have favorites, but that's not the way to treat any human being, especially an innocent child.

What she didn't know is that when I visited her and if she was not at home and her husband was, I would be afraid to go into the house. It's a shame. Many young girls get blamed for things they are innocent of; I was one of them. When she confronted me, I was so shocked! I respected her, but at that moment I asked her, "What the hell are you talking about?" I was so confused. What I was hearing just did not make any sense.

When we are unjustly blamed, we sometimes shed tears on the inside that only God sees. I've heard stories of old men throwing themselves onto little girls. That shows they have no respect for themselves. It is a very disgraceful behavior and a shame. It is hideous, upsetting and unacceptable. It gets me angry. And the most hurtful thing is when children cannot even talk to anyone about it, because they are afraid of not being heard, and with that they suffer in silence.

Also, there are many people that suffer in silence, because it is easier for them than to talk about their painful experience. They also want to avoid being judged by others. It was no surprise to me, when a friend of mine told me about a woman, who was still carrying the emotional pain of suffering sexual abuse as a young girl. This awful experience caused her to lose her self-esteem and left her emotionally scarred for life. I'm sure her parents had no idea what was going on with their daughter.

Today a lot of us women who came out from our hideouts can now have a voice to speak up and say enough is enough, and to help others who are suffering and would love to speak out but don't know how to. Somebody has to take the lead. There are some situations in the world that might be getting worse, but we must also open our eyes and see, that some things have improved, and some are getting better. A lot of us did not have access to a telephone when we were children. Nowadays there is no excuse. Some parents who can afford it, have allowed their child to have their own cell phone, so they can communicate wherever they are. Some men think they can fool a poor young girl by offering her money, just to be with them. This is why in many cases, I believe that poverty is a crime.

This broken girl had no self esteem and never had a voice. She is now a grown woman looking for help, and she found someone that she can talk to. She can empty out those pent-up emotions that have been eating at her for years. This is why we shouldn't judge anyone. Everyone has a past they are not proud of, whether it was their fault or not. The best thing we can do for our children is to encourage them to talk because that freedom is taken away from most children; they become like a mouse. Instead of raising strong children, some of us raise children that are confused and emotionally scarred for life.

I grew up in a home where my parents always told us not to ask anyone for anything. If we had only one penny in our purse, we were supposed to behave like we had a hundred dollars. I've grown up with that mentality, and to me it's a good one. Everyone is different, and I can only speak for myself. When I had just come to Canada and wanted to send for my daughter, I called her father on the phone to ask him for help with the ticket. He was so upset, that he went as far as hanging up the phone on me. He had a good paying job with the company he worked for in Canada. This was the same man that got me pregnant at the age of seventeen, just around the time I was planning to go off to nursing school in England. When a father turns their back on their own child, especially when they need help, that child can grow up feeling something is wrong with them, and it can affect them in so many ways.

I remember a few months after I arrived in Canada, I was taking a morning walk and a gentleman came up to me, introduced himself. As we continued the conversation, he told me that he worked for a big company, and he lived in the neighborhood. I asked him if the company was hiring. He said he didn't think so, but to give him my number just in case, and he would call to let me know. I remember telling him I had a hair salon back in my country, and he told me he could open a beauty salon for me. One day my phone rang and it was him on the line telling me he wanted me to meet him at the bank because he had some money for me. I was so upset, I said, "Wrong person. I don't want your money. Have some respect for yourself." I sent him flying.

The bible tells me that my God promises to supply all of my needs according to his riches in glory through Christ Jesus. I don't want anything from the devil. I'm not saying that God can't use a person to help another person, but it is easy to know when a man is lusting at a woman. I worked hard to send for my children and that's one of the things I'm most proud of.

Chapter 35

Child Molester in the School

One of my daughters when she was five years old, she attended a private school. I would drop her off at school every morning and pick her up after school. She told me there was a man that used to come to the school, and he would not allow her to go out to play with the children. He would take her on his lap and touch her up. I asked her if she had told the teacher about it, and she said yes, but that the teacher did not say anything.

The next day, I waited to see if this child molester came to the school, but he didn't. I was planning to report him to the police, and I'm not sure why I didn't. I'm sure my daughter wasn't the first child who was molested by this man. I've heard of so many, even young children who have been molested by old men. It's ridiculous. This is an offence that must not be taken lightly. Although my daughter is an adult now, she still talks about it. I did not have a voice for myself or my children, but in sharing my experience, I hope to give others a voice. Guilt can take a toll on our lives. Some of the worst guilt we can feel as a parent, is the time when our children needed us the most and were not there for them.

Animals Look out for Their Young Ones

It is just amazing how most animals bond with their young ones and takes care of them. If animals can be hurt when their love ones are, how much more can we as human beings. Sometimes, a dog will bite you if you try touching their pups.

This story is quite amazing! At the same time, what I witnessed was quite emotional. I left my home one summer morning a few years ago, to attend a meeting with a social worker. Around that time, I wasn't working, so I was not the happiest person. I kept complaining about my situation and trying to figure out my own problems.

It was an extremely hot day, so I stood under a shady tree for a few minutes while admiring a mother duck strolling along with her ducklings. I thought they were so cute, as they stood on the sidewalk waiting for the traffic to slow down, so they could cross the road. One particularly impatient duckling, instead of waiting for her mother and siblings, decided she would try crossing on her own. I could see how worried the poor mother was, because she saw the danger her little one was in. She cried aloud! But sad to say it did not help. The little duckling didn't know better and refused to listen. And then came a vehicle and ran over it and that was the end of her little one. I got emotional and felt sad for Mother Duck and the rest of her children. They took it so hard that wherever they had been off to, lost its importance to them. Instead, they all turned right back and returned to stand under one of the trees and wept over their loved one. They all were just clucking and quacking.

There are many lessons that we can learn from this story. I never took it lightly. It may be that the Lord wanted me to learn something from what happened that day. I shared it with the social worker and told her how I was feeling before I saw what happened to the ducks. She thought that maybe God wanted me to learn something from it, and that He was telling me not to worry, that everything would be all right.

I reflected on Matthew 6:25 where Jesus says,

"Therefore, I say unto you, take no thought for your life, what you shall eat or what you shall drink; nor yet for your body what you shall put on, Is not the life more than meat, and the body than raiment?"

Despite all the challenges that we may have encountered in life, the gift of life is wonderful, and is worth fighting for. We need to fight for our children. If we don't who will? Sometimes when my daughter talks about her childhood experience, I can hear the emotions in her voice. There are some flashbacks that can slow us down and cause us to not enjoy life the way we should.

Pent-Up Emotions Can Be Dangerous

I believe some people are very good at hiding their emotions, which is not always a good thing. Those pent-up emotions can eat a person up on the inside. I have worked with people who are so broken, just waiting to empty their emotions out. You can almost feel their pain. When a person feels nauseated, then vomits, they feel better. When we can talk about what's bothering us, or even cry it out, we feel better. Sometimes, finding a support group helps.

Suffering in silence can do a whole lot of damage to a person, and it sometimes affects their ability to take care of themselves and even maintain a relationship. We experience emotions when we talk about a problem that is bothering us. This is quite normal in the healing process. When I decided to go to counselling, I thought it was a good place to strip off the mask and start my healing journey. I was like a pregnant woman experiencing contractions. I couldn't wait to get my feelings out. I had so much to talk about.

On my first day, I was able to talk about some of the things that were tearing me up on the inside. I cried through the whole session which lasted for about forty-five minutes. Somehow, I was disappointed, as I was expecting more. It was my first time going for counselling. After the first session, I said to myself, if that is what counselling is, I don't need it. To me it didn't make any sense. I was expecting that the counselor would try to understand the pain I was feeling, and that he would at least give me some advice. Instead, he was just staring at me, and listening while I kept talking and crying my heart out.

Pain from Helping Others

I believe caring for others is the example that Christ has set for us to follow. We all would love to know when we do a good deed for someone, that the end results will be a good and pleasant one, but sad to say, too often, it brings us pain. Not knowing the outcome of something could be alarming. Sometimes we feel sorry for a person and take on a responsibility that we shouldn't.

My son and I are so much alike. A few years ago, he asked me to help a friend of his who attended the same school with him. Apparently, this young man had no place to live at the time. He was fifteen years old, just one year older than my son. I thought, well, showing some compassion to this boy cannot be wrong in the sight of God. So, I took him in and treated him as my own son. I fed him, made him feel comfortable and gave him a bed to sleep in when night came. I realized he had some emotional issues. I thought the best thing was to invite him to church, and have the pastor pray for him. I wanted the best for this young man.

My son took him as a brother, and we both believed that we were doing the right thing by taking him into our house to help him. He got himself into problems for silly things and while at work one day, I got a call from authorities asking me if I could give consent for him, by saying he would be residing at my house. Again, trying to help, I said yes, not knowing I was setting myself up for trouble. I must say I had some painful experience with him. It can be heart breaking when you try helping people and all they bring you in the end is heartaches.

At that time, if I had a husband, I believe he would have talked me out of taking on such responsibility. Sometimes we need another pair of eyes, to help guide us, and to see what we cannot see. And, it is obvious if his parent put him out means he wasn't behaving himself. I decided to call his mother one day to let her know her son was staying at my house. I thought this way, at least she would be happy to know that he was safe and had a place to sleep and food to eat. Instead, she told me I was spoiling and encouraging him. Well, I felt offended. When I got off the phone, I was wondering what she meant when she said I was spoiling him. But then I realized that she was only trying to teach her son a lesson.

The lesson I learned from this experience, is that I need to be more cautious. I cannot always allow my compassionate heart to trick me into thinking that I must help everyone. In spite of it all, I believe this young man, even when he gets old, will always remember the love and compassion that my son and I showed him in a time when he needed help. When you can show a true reflection of who Jesus Christ is, thats how you bring glory to God.

Glorifying God in The Midst of Pain

How can a person glorify the Lord in the midst of pain? I was invited to a week-long meeting in New York with the pastor of Open Heaven Ministries and a group of women from the church. I believe this helped me to stay focused and to numb the emotional pain I was feeling. We had to get up early every morning to pray and prepare for the evening church service. The first night, the pastor called on me to sing. I remember singing the song "Jesus You promised never to leave me." The congregation was moved with emotion, and the pastor encouraged me to keep on singing for the Lord.

Shortly after that, Pastor Cyrus called on me to pray for the church, and for another sister to pray for the women of the church. I was a bit apprehensive and wondered, of all the women in the group, why he'd called on me. Then I remembered him saying he'd never do anything without first consulting God. In my mind, I said, "Lord, if You told him to call on me to pray for the church, you will put the words in my mouth." I have never experienced anything like what happened that night at church. As I began to pray, the congregation joined in, and there was a mighty move of the Holy Spirit. It felt like the place was shaking and that things were breaking in the air.

On the last night of the meeting, we all received gifts from the church members. I wish we had extended our stay for another week, as we had such a great time! After that, I still had to deal with the pain, accompanied by some unresolved issues; that made it hard for me to maintain an emotional balance. Surprisingly, I found myself right back in the counsellor's office, and this time she asked some leading questions. With the little knowledge I had about counsellors, I never knew that they were not allowed to give advice, and this to me didn't make any sense at all. However, I was able to empty out the bottled-up emotions that I felt, and at least it helped me to transition from the place where I've been stuck for many years.

After six sessions, I decided to not continue, so I sent my counsellor a thank you card telling him how much I appreciated his help. I knew that the ball was in my court and how I played it would determine the results. I had to start taking control of my life.

I knew of a woman who said she'd been going to counselling for over twenty years. To me, that is quite a long time. There are people who feel they cannot survive on their own after being hit by the storms of life. Some people feel they need ongoing counselling because of what they have been through. After the woman had shared with me some of the things that she had been through, I then had a better understanding of why she was in counselling all those years. No one should tell a person how long they should be in therapy. It is entirely up to them. Again, some people are so broken that they need constant help in order for them to get through life.

I believe it is crucial that a person seeks counselling if they are carrying around pent-up emotions.

Chapter 36
I Thought He was Sent by God

After I arrived in Canada, I tried calling my husband a couple of times, but never was able to get him. I left a couple of messages, but he never returned the call. I was planning on giving him a trip to Canada in hopes of reconciliation. I know that sounds crazy. Yes it is. I can't even believe myself. Sometimes God makes the way for us to escape from a bad situation, and we still try to find ourselves right back in the mess.

I met Charmin a few months after I arrived in Canada, through his brother who was a bishop. I was in my thirties and he was in his fifties. I remember a friend of mine had bought a new car, and she mentioned the idea of us paying him a visit just around summertime. He lived in a beautiful apartment. It was well put together, and everything seemed to be in place. He seemed to have it all together. It took me a while before I could commit to a relationship, because it was not love at first sight. He knew all the right things to say and do.

He invited me out to dinner, took me shopping, showed up at my door with red roses and made me feel like a queen. I felt like it was the best thing that had happened to me and I thanked God for sending me this man. After coming out of an abusive marriage, I could not believe this moment was really happening. I said to God, "If this is of you, thank you father."

I had never felt love in my life like this before. It felt so good, so real, that I refused to think he was not sent by God. This also helped me to get over my husband. When I was at his house, he allowed me to answer his phone, saying when it rang there was nothing for him to hide. One day though, when I did answer the phone, it was a woman on the other end of the line asking to speak with Charmin. He took the phone and told her not to call him back, that he didn't want to be with her anymore. He asked me if I was happy that he told her that. I said no, because you could end up treating me the same way. However, things were still good between us, until one day another woman called. Again, I asked who was calling, she said it was his girlfriend. I was about to tell her I was his girlfriend, but he ripped the phone cord from the receiver. That was valid proof he was cheating. After that, I knew I could not trust him.

As time went by, breaking up and making up became the thing between us. He did and said some things that made me realize I was dealing with an emotional unstable man who had suffered hurts and disappointments in his past relationships. He decided to put me to the test one day by spreading a thousand dollars on his bed and leaving me at his apartment while he went off to work. He acted so surprised when he got home and found the thousand dollars exactly where he had left it. He said he could not believe I did not touch his money. He spoke from the experience that he had with other women.

When my divorce came through in 1991, I thought I would be getting ready to walk down the aisle. Instead, it was time to walk away from the relationship. I was so disappointed in myself that I had wasted two years in a relationship I thought was going someplace, only to realize it had come to an end.

I locked myself in a closet and cried my heart out to God. I cried so much that I felt like I was drinking my tears. I felt like I had disappointed my heavenly father and I asked him to forgive me for the two years I had wasted with this man. I was always looking forward to the day when Charmin and I would make it right. It was just an elusive dream. At that point, I realized that all that glitters is not gold. I believe one of the things that fooled me, is when I heard he was from a Christian background.

I found myself sinking into deep self-pity, and again the pity party went on for years. Charmin wasted no time. Shortly after we broke up, I heard he got married and divorced. Some men move on quickly while some of us women sit with a broken heart hoping that they will come back knocking someday. It is possible that if Charmin had decided to come back I would have given him another chance, with the intention of him repairing the damage he had done to my pride and self-esteem.

Right before we broke up, I remember him telling me any woman he gets involved with, he would just use them. I did not want this man to keep going around hurting women. I cannot imagine how many women get played by men like these. There are times when revenge comes with smooth talk. And with that, it takes a long time before you find out it was only another spider that was trying to pull you into his web.

Satan will disguise himself well. And not knowing it, we fall for his evil devices. He then preys on us and leaves us wounded and broken. Not only that, we become so afraid and start thinking that every man on the earth is just waiting to disgrace us. Some women on the other hand run into the arms of another man hoping that they will find rescue and help them to heal. Sometimes it works for some, and sometimes it makes matters worse.

After many heartbreaks, it becomes difficult trusting someone. I believe it is wise to seek the Lord before pursuing a relationship. We may think that the safest place to find a partner is the church. And while that can be true, sad to say, the enemy has a way of disguising and showing up anywhere, and Church is no exception. When I was a teenager, I heard of a man who visited a church and met a young Christian woman and they both fell in love. She got pregnant with his first child, no marriage, the second child came and when she asked him about marriage, he said to her, "If Jesus you love so much you disappointed him who is me." I can't imagine how that girl felt.

It is important that we ask the Holy Spirit for guidance before pursuing any relationship. Jesus told Simon, that Satan desired to have him, that he may sift him like wheat, but he will pray that his faith will not fail. (Luke 22: 31-32) The enemy is not our friend, he will use anyone and anything to get to the child of God. He wants to sift us like wheat. Thank God that Jesus is at the right hand of the father making intercessions for us. He tells us we must be "vigilant, be sober, because our adversary the enemy is going around seeking whom he may devour." (1Peter 1: 8-9). I cant believe I was now feeling like a fool, after being treated like a queen.

I needed to do something to feel better about myself, so I enrolled at the Art and Technique Hairstyling School to do an advanced course in hairstyling. It was in 1997, five years after I broke up with Charmin. One morning on my way to school God saved me from getting knocked out by a beer bottle that was thrown from the seventeenth floor of the building where I lived. It came so close, it was about a quarter of an inch from hitting me, and smashed into pieces. I was so shaken up, you should have seen the drama, as the tears were streaming down my face. I wasn't aware that some teenagers were drinking, and throwing bottles. I was going about my own business never troubling anyone. I went back to my apartment crying. My son was worried and asked what was wrong. Then I told him what happened. I asked where is God in all this? He said Mom, is obvious that God had his angels around you, that is why you did not get hit with the bottle. At that horrifying moment I couldn't see it, but when I heard those words from him, I knew he was right. I realized I should be thanking God instead of being upset with him. Think about how many times God uses our own children and others to remind us of how good he is. The course ran for ten months, and at the end of the course I applied for a job with a beauty salon, working as an apprentice and making six dollars an hour. I quit within two months and decided to look for work at another hair salon. And that also, was not working out, so I decided to apply at a clothing store, making nine dollars and twenty-five cents an hour. Although the pay was not that favorable, I liked my job, as I got to dress up and feel good about myself. I looked forward to going to my job every day, as a sales representative. The manager was a wonderful young Christian woman and we got along fine. If I was not having a good day, she would sit and talk with me in her office and pray with me. She was such a blessing.

CHAPTER 37

The Journey of a Single Parent

Changing light bulbs, tightening screws and playing the part of two parents is not easy. I often wonder how some single women do it and keep it together. Single parenting is an emotional process, and if you do not have to do it alone, don't. There were times I wish I had a good man with me on this journey. There were times my children wish they had their father around to love them and to give their Mommy a break. Children not having their father in their lives feel like something is wrong with them. And they will always have questions even when they become adults. It takes a lot of patience for a woman to raise her children on her own, not having a partner. The important thing was knowing that I was there for them. That is what counts, even though at times it was rough and lonely. And, if you ask me if it was frightening at times, I would say, "Yes."

We cannot erase the fact that children growing up need two parents. My children and I cried together, laughed together, sang together and at times watched children's shows together. My son and I enjoyed watching *Little House on the Prairie*. All these were precious moments. Children all grow up so fast. I wish I was able to go back and change the times when I would thump and yell at them out of frustration. I could have handled situations better if I had only asked God for wisdom and understanding. We also need to understand our children and what they are feeling.

When my son asked a question I was not prepared for, like,

"Where is my father in all this?" it would only explain the full extent of the pain he was feeling of not having a father in his life. He always used to pray and hope that his father would show up, especially when he turned fourteen.

But, unfortunately, it never happened, and that left him quite disappointed. He said by then he started losing hope.

The age of fourteen is when most children are going through changes in their lives. This is when they need a lot of guidance and support. Boys need their father to help them make good decisions and to help in choosing their friends wisely. There is also the peer pressure that most of them must deal with. Fourteen is the age when many girls get pregnant and don't have a clue what is going on. When I was fourteen and heard that my father was on vacation from England, I was excited to visit him, as I did not see him for seven years. On my second visit, I wanted to ask him for twenty dollars that I needed so badly to buy some school accessories. I mentioned it to my stepmother, but she said to me, when a child is already grown, they should not look to their father for help. I couldn't believe what I was hearing. It bugged me for many years. I was only a fourteen-year-old girl, who wanted to have a father daughter relationship, which every girl would love to have. And what she said to me, makes me think that she was only talking out of jealousy.

I remember when they were living in England, on about two or three occasions he sent me a few dollars and I was quite grateful for it. Still, this couldn't make up for all the years that my mom had to be doing it on her own. When children are hurting and faced with difficult situations in their own lives, they need both parents to be there for them. I experienced some difficult times in my teenage years. No alcohol, no smoking, but I suffered abuse in different ways. Parents sometimes have no idea the things that their children go through. If some of us only knew more than what we already know, the advantage that was taken on our children, we would fall sick. My dad was not around when I needed him. I got blamed for things I knew nothing about. Defending myself seems like it was the most difficult thing to do.

As an adult when I'm faced with difficult situations in my life, I ask my heavenly Father, "God where are you in all this?" just as my son asked me where his father was in all this. Many times, I had conversations with myself, saying, "Barbara, you do not have to do it alone. Find yourself a man." But, then I thought, if it was that easy to go out there and find a good man, a lot of struggling women would not be single. One of the things I regret, and I ask myself, is why I allowed my children's father to get off the hook so easy.

I never knew what it was to take their father to court for child support, and when I looked back, I realized how naive I was for not taking such action. I felt guilty and foolish. I asked myself, "What kind of woman are you?" I felt like a failure in the eyes of my children, even though they did not look at me that way. But, when the pity party starts and they do not understand, that is another thing.

Dealing with a broken heart and still being tough for your children at the same time is not easy. It is not easy while your heart is tearing up to the point where you feel so overwhelmed that you don't know what to do. Those of us who have done single parenting realize it takes a lot of courage and patience. At times, I became weak in the process. There were times my two youngest would fight and I really felt, "Okay, this is it." I would yell at the top of my voice and feel like I was losing it, as unkind words spilled out of my mouth. I would regret it afterwards. They were good children. All they needed was a good father to love and care for them as their mommy did. But it was certainly no fault of their own. No child brings themselves into this world. And when my son asked me if I brought him into the world to see trouble, I understood his pain. And my heart ached.

The choices we make at times if we are not careful, can affect our children and cripple us for the rest of our lives if we allow them to. Without a steady income, many times I had to use credit cards to buy clothes and food for my children. A couple of times, when things were rough, I called the Salvation Army to help me out with some food, so my children would not go to bed hungry. Not having bus fare, I carried heavy bags through the freezing cold, walking over two miles to and from home. I remember bringing home a whole lot of tin stuff, which I would not normally buy, and one day my son said to me, "Mom, you do not buy tin stuff. How come you buy them now?"

Oh, children keep a tag on what you do. I was ashamed to let my children know I went to the food bank. The second time, I could not hide it. My conscience would not allow me to tell a lie. The lady who worked at the food bank was a nice Christian person. I told her how I felt, and she said she understood, but that l should look at it as a blessing. And, yes, she was right. I guess I allowed pride to keep me from seeing it as a blessing. I was allowed once a month. I remember just around the Christmas holiday I received a box with groceries from one of the churches. It was quite a surprise. I must have filled out a form and couldn't remember.

At that time a family member was at my house and for some reason I felt bad, even though I was grateful. I remember putting ten dollars in an envelope and mailing it out to the church thanking them for helping me out that Christmas. A few days after, I remember having a conversation with the same family member about how I felt not having a job. To my great surprise, I was told that I was lazy. I can't tell you how much that hurt my feelings. That person wasn't around when I had to be working different jobs and two jobs in one day to get my children to Canada. Some people love to judge you, all because they are in a better position than you, forgetting where they were and that you were the one that helped them. It doesn't matter how nice you treat them, they always find a way to hurt your feelings. I thank God, after two months I was blessed with a job, and I did not have to go back to the food bank. I began to regain my independence once more and started feeling better about myself. My children were happy to know that their mother did not have to go back to the food bank, and that I was working again.

My youngest daughter would say to me that she would feel jealous when other girls talked about their dads taking them shopping. She wished she had a dad who would also take her shopping. We need to let our children know we are there for them, by giving them the attention they need at times and by praying for them. I never cease praying for my children. Now, they are all grown, and have children of their own. I remember my son saying he would break the cycle and make sure he is there for his children. I must say he is a good father and a good son.

I'm a blessed and proud grandmother, and I love all my grandchildren very much. I enjoy taking my two younger granddaughters to church and shopping. I love when they walk through the aisles looking for cute little summer dresses, and then they go into separate fitting rooms and come out modelling them for me to see. I love to see the joy on their little faces when I take them to McDonald's, their favorite place. And, hearing them say, "I love you. You are the best grandma," thrills my heart.

The funniest thing is sometimes the younger one makes a comment about my hair, saying, "Grandmas don't wear those hairstyles," or she makes a funny joke about grandmas. She loves playing hide and seek. It reminds me of when I was her age. And, when she says, "Grandma, come, let's play hide and seek." I say, "Grandmas don't play hide and seek." She laughs and says, "You are a young grandma. You can play hide and seek."

There is a saying that grandchildren keep you young. I know one day they will grow up and become adults and I will wish they were small again. We must thank God for the blessings of our children and grandchildren. We need to enjoy them, as they all grow up so fast. I look at my grandson Jaeden who is now a teenager, and I can't believe how fast he has grown. I remember when he was just four years old, he had the chicken pox, and one morning he was praying and giving thanks for everything around him, including a blue flashlight that he had on the dresser in the room. The most interesting thing I heard this child say was, "Thank you God for the chicken pox." This amazed me!

The apostle Paul encourages us in, 1 Thessalonians 5:18 *"That we should give thanks in all circumstances, for it is the will of God."* I believe God was teaching me something from Jaeden's prayer. The hardest thing to do is to give thanks for sickness and problems. There are times when I'm confused about something I don't understand, instead of complaining, "I say thank you Lord." and Hallelujah anyhow. I know Jaeden was born with a gift. I was asked to preach at a small church one Sunday morning, and I got up that day with a terrible toothache. My gums were swollen, I could hardly open my mouth to speak. I did not know what to do.

I thought at the last moment it would look bad to call the pastor to tell him I'm unable to make it, when he is already depending on me. I asked my little Jaeden to pray for me. "He said OK, Grandma, let us bow our heads and clasp our hands. "He prayed, Lord Jesus, please heal this little kink in Grandma Gum Amen." He had gotten straight to the point. That childlike faith and short prayer did it! Immediately the pain left, and the swelling was gone, and my gum was healed. I was so happy! I immediately jumped out of bed, headed for the shower, got dressed, had some breakfast, and went off to church. God heard and answered the prayer of an innocent child.

(Matthew 18:3) *"Except you become as a little child you cannot enter the kingdom of heaven."*

Children have faith and believe without doubting. They have a clean heart and hold no grudges. Therefore, Jesus wants us to change the way we think and become as a child. Some people need to let go of all the grudges they hold against others. This could be one of the reasons some prayers are not answered. Un-belief is also an insult to God. When we doubt God, it means that we don't believe in his word.

The bible says (Hebrews 11:6) *"But without faith it is impossible to please Him. For he that cometh to God must believe that He is, and that He is a rewarder of those who diligently seek Him."*

In 2004, just a week before the tsunami happened in Indonesia, I remember one morning Jaeden had a vision while he was praying, and suddenly, he opened his eyes, in amazement. From the look on his face, I could see he was quite surprised! He said, "Grandma, how come I saw America while I was praying?" Maybe God wants me to pray for America. I was very much surprised like he was. I said really! You saw America? He said, "Yes grandma, I saw America while I was praying." I said to him, I believe God wants you to pray for America." God uses children in different ways. We can learn a lot from them. I'm sure if I remind my grandson about these things, he may not remember, because he was only a four-year old.

Chapter 38

Who is That Woman in the Mirror?

I could not believe, when I looked in the mirror. "Barbara is that you?" All I could see was a woman in misery. I was so unhappy. I would look at myself, cry and pull my hair. I could hear a voice saying, "Look at you. Nothing is working for you. You are just a failure." And, I would believe it. I can't believe the crazy thoughts that honked my mind, as Satan kept tumbling my emotions.

I was on edge all the time. I did not want to socialize. I would come up with a lame excuse every time someone invited me out. It was difficult for me to accept a compliment. Church is where I always wanted to be. It was the place where I could really let my emotions out. I remember being in the prayer line one Sunday, with tears streaming down my face, and the pastor said to me, "God will give you beauty for ashes." I had all the signs of depression.

One day, I envisioned three glasses of juice and thought how easy it would be to put something in them and have the children and I drink it, and we would be out of here. That was a plan of Satan, who saw me as a threat and his aim was to destroy me.

This happened just a few months after I preached my first sermon on ladies Sunday at Open Heaven Ministries. It was so powerful, that there wasn't a dry eye in church. People responded to the conviction of the Holy Spirit and, after giving an Altar call they all came forward and rededicated their lives to Jesus Christ. After I was finished preaching, some people were asking if anybody taped the sermon. It was truly a blessing. That must have made the devil furious.

Chapter 39

The Couch Became My Best Friend

It was the Christmas season. My sister made Christmas dinner and she invited me and the children over, but, I did not feel like going. The couch was my comfort zone. The children thought it would be better for me to go with them, than for me to sit in my pity party all day long. Eventually, I got up off the couch, got dressed and decided to join them. I must say that we all enjoyed ourselves, and I had no regrets. My sister had a box packed with gifts and everyone had to plunge into the box and take one. When I unwrapped mine, it was a beautiful ornament shaped like a bible, with the Lord's prayer. I believe it was God's way of reminding me that he is with me always.

Early in the morning, I would make for the bushes, where no one could see or hear me, and I would cry my heart out to God. I remember kneeling on a stone and crying out to God, for help. I thought I needed to see a psychologist, but I did not have the money, so I asked my doctor to refer me to a psychiatrist instead. I was prepared to tell him everything that was going on. I was disappointed when he quickly scribbled a prescription as if to say he had no time to listen to me. Within less than a minute I was out of his office. All I wanted him to do was give me a few minutes of his time. I just wanted to cry my heart out.

He put me on Paxil and another medication. I did not want to have to rely on them to fix my problems, and apart from that, the medications had too many side effects. It made me feel tired and sleepy all the time and my mouth was always dry. I had lost my appetite. I am normally a slim person, but I lost so much weight on those medications that the one pair of jeans I wore most of the time were falling off me.

One day, a young man in the prayer group I was in, advised me to get rid of those medications, and to trust God for my healing and deliverance. He told me he had an accident, and the doctor had put him on one of those medications. He used to be sleepy every time he knelt to pray, and he believed it was a trick of the enemy to keep him from praying, so he got rid of the medication. As soon as I got home that night from church, I went to the shelf, reached for them and threw them in the garbage. I would not advise anyone to stop taking their medication at any point, except with the advice of your physician. One day, when I was feeling the blues, I went back looking for them, forgetting I had thrown them away. The enemy was playing with my mind. I went and knelt beside my bed and began to have a serious talk with God! He told me to get a pen and paper and to begin to write. I started writing and was surprised to see things like anger, fear, unforgiveness, and guilt. I asked, "Really, Lord, do I have these things in me?" He said, "Give them all to me." God knows us much more than we know ourselves.

It was then I realized these destructive spirits controlled my life, and that they were lying dormant. I asked God to forgive those who inflicted pain on me and my children. I knew that is what he wanted me to do, yet it was difficult for me. But then, the scripture hit me, where Jesus was on the cross, and he reminded me that even with all the suffering and pain he endured, he still asked the father to forgive them, for they know not what they do. Right there and then, I had the choice to forgive or to not forgive. I would say I forgive and then find myself back into the same situation time and time again, my emotions try to get the best of me.

Chapter 40

Life Controlled by Fear

My life was controlled by fear, tormenting me for years. I was afraid to make decisions, afraid to make plans, afraid of the unknown. I kept living in the past, allowing life to pass me by. I was too broken and consumed with self-pity, and I kept beating myself up. One Sunday evening, I visited a church and met a pastor who had flown in from Florida to preach that Sunday. I thought I should ask him to pray for me, but before I could open my mouth, my tears did the talking. When I did eventually open my mouth, all I kept saying was, I'm so tired. I was overwhelmed by everything that was going on in my life.

I remember, after he finished preaching, he asked his prayer team to pray for me. They all surrounded me and prayed. I felt the peace came over me. Afterwards, they all hugged me, and one sister said to me, "At times, all we need is a hug." I can tell you, I needed much more than that. I needed a miracle. I needed to start living, instead of just existing. While a hug goes a long way, there are times some people need more than that. I needed someone to listen to me and to at least try to understand what I was going through, but not having walked in my shoes, no one would ever understand.

There was another small church I used to attend, called the Intercultural Worship Centre. One night, after service, I asked the pastor of that church to pray for me. I remember him rebuking the spirit of depression from my life. When I got home, I knew something had happened. I knew God was at work. I never ceased praying. I never ceased going to church. I remained positive. One day, as I was in my kitchen doing dishes, the Holy Spirit gave me a beautiful song, entitled, "Jesus, You Are All I Need." Joy flooded my heart and I knew it was my song of deliverance. I ran for my tape recorder and recorded it. This reminded me of the Psalms where David said,

> *"I waited upon the Lord patiently and he inclined to my prayer. He took me out of a horrible pit, put a new song in my mouth, plant my feet upon a rock and he established my going." Psalms 40:1-2*

The enemy never give up. I had to keep resisting him, every time he tried to bombard my mind. He would try his best in all ways to bring me back down into the pit of depression. My children would say to me, "Mom, you cannot continue beating up on yourself. You have to take care of yourself. Come on mom, you are a strong woman." Hearing those words from them gave me lots of courage and strength to go on. I knew I must take a stand and fight back. I realized I was good at encouraging others, and at times I also needed encouragement.

In John 8:36, Jesus said this. *"Whom the son sets free is free indeed."*

It doesn't mean that the enemy (the devil) wouldn't try his schemes with you, but you must take a stand for what you know, and what you believe. And when he comes to speak lies to you, have your sword ready for him which is the word of God. James 4:7 says, "Submit yourselves, then, to God, Resist the devil and he will flee from you". We must stand our ground, and confess the word knowing and believing that we are set free according to God's word. When the devil went to tempt Jesus in the wilderness, Jesus had to resist him three times.

The third time Jesus said to him, "It is written again, thou shalt not tempt the Lord thy God, and him only shall thou serve." Then the devil left him. (Matthew 4:7) Jesus set the example for us to follow. We must let the devil know, it is written that whom JESUS, set free is free in indeed! Knowing that the Lord had already set me free from depression, I could not allow my emotions to have control over me anymore. Satan will play on your emotions, to get you confused, and cause you to doubt God. I also realize for me to make my life better, I must stay focused, so I can help someone else. It is the only way to fulfill what the Lord will have me to do. When God delivers you, it is a new day in your life, and you can start living again, and dreaming again.

You just cannot sit around waiting for things to happen. This is the opportunity to testify and share the good news, so that others will know what God has done for you he can also do it for them. The word of God says, we overcome by the word of our testimony." God wants to use us to bless others.

Life sometimes is like climbing a slippery pole. Years ago, I had a dream that I was trying to climb a hill and I couldn't get a grip because the hill was extremely slippery. Eventually, when I did get a grip, I couldn't go an inch further. It was difficult for me to get another one. The strangest thing about that dream is, I found myself lying on my back, going backwards down the hill. So weird! And, there was a man at the bottom of the hill, he picked me up and he said to me, you will talk about this. God already knew the things I would encounter in my life, and that I would be writing this book and sharing my testimony, encouraging others on this journey of life. Whatever problems you are facing in your life, sometimes shows up in your dream.

Don't Waste Time

I have come to realize how much time I have wasted focusing on the wrongs that people did to me, not thinking, that it was only doing me more harm than good. By now we should understand that some people never change.

They are fixed in their own ways, and what we think and feel doesn't make a difference to them. So, we are the ones who must move on with our lives and make ourselves happy. I remember there was a time I asked someone about something they did that really hurt me. Instead, she brushed me off and walked away. I can tell you it hurts. I felt like a fool. It is not the first-time this has happened. To me, when people hurt you and don't care, it means that they are also experiencing pain themselves, and they look for someone to take revenge on, which is unfair. It is a cruel thing to do. I believe there are ways a person could deal with their pain instead of using it on others. It is not the first time I was hurt by people I loved and helped.

To be honest, If you have confronted someone that hurt you to tell them how you feel, and they ignored you, then find another way. Try writing a note and slip it into their purse or pants pocket. That is only if its really bothering you. At the end of the day, you are the one that is feeling the pain. You can only stifle your feelings for so long, and pretending all is well, until one day you realize this thing is eating at you, because you never dealt with it in the first place. It can label stress on your heart and affect you in different ways. You must let the person know what they did is not acceptable. This may not change anything, because some people hurt your feelings and don't care. Therefore, nothing you say to them will make a difference. You will at least feel a lot better. The people that are upfront are the ones that gain respect from others and survive better in the world. It is never too late to stand up and speak out for your right.

I remember having a conversation one day with a beautiful lady. I never knew how angry and broken she was until she shared certain things with me. It was unbelievable.

This a is a true saying. "Never judge a book by the cover." To hear her boasting of the way she treated someone that she should at least show some compassion to, makes me wonder how many people are walking around with pent-up emotions, and a tearful heart. From then I learned that this poor lady, she was just another one of the saddies that was walking around with a pretty masque pretending all is well. I am not saying that Christians must be a walk over, but it is important we maintain a good standard.

Although it is not always easy keeping your emotions under control, at the same time, we must exercise self-control. Life is unpredictable at times. We never know what situation we may find ourselves in. The same person we treat like an outcast, some day we may need their help. If we love the Lord Jesus, we will show it by the way we treat others.

Chapter 41

Grenada: 1983 Invasion

War broke out on the Island of Grenada in October 1983, and the United States invaded. It was quite frightening to see soldiers with rifles hiding in bushes and camping near houses in the neighborhood. I was terrified. I was pregnant with my youngest daughter. I remember hearing gunshots, and that scared the hell out of me. Some soldiers were jumping with parachutes. I had never witnessed anything like that before.

My husband was scared like hell too. That day he went to the kitchen to grab something to eat and saw a soldier pointing up his rifle towards the window, and he dashed back into the bedroom shaking like a leaf. He went and laid on the bed and I was hiding under it. In fright, we both reached out our hands to each other and began to pray and ask God to please keep us safe. That was the only time I could recall my husband praying with me. I could tell he was terrified.

Looting was taking place all over the city of Saint George's and every place of business was closed. We heard of people walking away with fridges, telephones, televisions, you name it. After a couple of days, when the curfew was lifted, soldiers were lined up on both sides of the road, rifles in hand. I was still terrified having to walk past them, but they were quite friendly. What a relief. I could see the happiness on people's faces as they shouted in celebration, "God bless Uncle Reagan!" By October 15th, Grenadians were ready to get back on their feet.

Chapter 42

Watch out for the Boys

Can you imagine walking down the road minding your own business, and having someone disrespect you calling you nasty names, for no reason? Many young girls have been through that horrific experience. Girls would become apprehensive as they approached the block where the enemy sent his agents out to work. Boys there were just waiting to harass girls, and I was not exempted from that treatment. They enjoyed saying nasty things that would make a girl feel like she was the worst thing God had ever created on this Earth. Their approach was with no respect. Though they knew your name, they would call out, "You, girl," if I ignored them. They would disrespect me and embarrass me in the presence of their friends.

Some words could pierce a person right through to their heart and leave them wounded. This may sound like a joke, but it is quite true. It caused many of us to walk with a limp. My oldest daughter said to me she was so wounded by those words, and there are times she finds herself walking with a limp. My feet went out of gear from the minute I laid eyes on those boys. I cannot believe the kind of insults and emotional abuse we had to go through as young teenage girls. Some girls have lost their self-esteem and cannot hold their head up because of this terrible experience.

The boys would tell horrible lies and make others believe things that were not true. They would use the most disgusting obscene language and they would get away with it. Things like that could completely damage a girl for life. Through those brutal experiences, I learned that when people do not feel good about themselves, they try putting another person down. Some of these people never made any headway in life. It is a sad thing, that some people provoke others to anger. Innocent people go to jail because of being provoked by someone.

Not everyone is able to exercise self-control in those kinds of situations. I never knew how to stand up for my rights. Too many times I allowed people to tell me what they wanted and to treat me how they wanted. What I have come to realize though, is that we are living in a world where there is a lot of hatred, envy and jealousy among people, which is sad. We don't have to be like everyone else. We can make a difference, and "Shine the light for everyone to see."

When people provoke your peace and try to damage your self-esteem, some day they will reap the repercussion of their own evil doing. This is a true saying, if you do good, good will follow you.

Chapter 43

Afraid to Be Happy

Afraid to be happy? Why would a person be afraid of happiness? That is insane and just doesn't make sense. Well let's find out. When things are going fine, you feel that there is nothing to worry about, until something comes and interrupts your life, and just before you get a break, something else comes to shake the life out of you. You begin to wonder what the heck is going on? You then ask yourself the question, why is all this happening to me?

After many years of experiencing problems that brought on emotional stress, I was afraid to be happy. I thought that pain and misery were all life had to offer me, so after a while I began to look at all the abuse and disappointments that I've been through as normal. I would say, "Oh well, I guess that's what life is. Others have been through it." Every time I felt like I was getting a breakthrough, I would start getting worried and wondering what was next.

One day, a young woman in her twenties was browsing through the store where I was working. Surprisingly, she said to me, that because of the disappointments and hurts she experienced in her life, she was afraid to be happy. My response was, I thought it was I alone who felt that way! When we allow the pain of the past to hold us captive, it is a very sad thing. The rapists, the ones who told humongous lies, the ones who accused us, they all moved on with their lives, while we sit in the slump feeling sorry for ourselves.

As my daughter would say, "The people who hurt us are fluffing up their pillow when the night comes and having their eight- and nine-hours sleep, and their full three course meal." When we give the things they have done to us, power over us, then, yes, we will be afraid of relationships, and rob ourselves of happiness. We will think that we are the unhappiest human beings on Earth and life will keep passing us by.

One evening, after work, I decided to go to Chapters bookstore to wait for my friend to finish work, so I could get a ride home with him. As I entered the store, a book about how to find peace and happiness in this world, caught my eyes. " Surprisingly, as I looked across from where I was standing, there was about five people sitting on a bench with the very same book in their hands. I was encouraged by that, as it helped me to know I was not the only one looking for answers. I came to realize though, that the only place we can find peace is in Jesus Christ. He is our peace. Even though we may be troubled about what is going on around us, we can still have peace, as he gave me when my daughter was in the intensive care unit at the hospital. He has offered the peace to us, which surpasses all understanding. When you get to that place where you are afraid to be happy, that's a spiritual attack from hell. Everyone wants to be happy. I believe if happiness was available in the stores, you would not find any on the shelves.

(See Philippians 4:7) *"And the peace of God which transcends all understanding,* will *guard your hearts and your mind in Christ Jesus."*

Things happen to everyone in this world. Life has its ups and downs. We cannot depend on another person for our happiness. If we don't learn to love ourselves, we cannot enjoy the life that God has ordained for us to live. Sometimes we settle for things that brings us pain instead of fulfillment. Fear is a spirit and we must not allow it to control our life.

Chapter 44

Not Her Fault

One study estimated, that thirty seven percent of women experience physical and sexual abuse before the age of twenty-one. Another research study showed that it could be a higher percentage.

From my experience, taking a person at face value is not enough for an evaluation. Some men paint a bad picture for the innocent ones. There are still some good ones out there, but it is difficult for us as women to differentiate. For example, if a woman asked a co-worker for a ride home after work, knowing he was going the same direction as her, you wouldn't think for a second, that he would pull into some out of the way place and force himself on her. We have other incidents of women being sexually assaulted by their boss, or by a best friend's brother or someone else. How would that be the woman's fault. I have no doubt that rape victims suffer depression and anxiety from time to time.

A high percentage of babies have been born out of rape. Some men are good at covering up, and some of us women help them to do that. Some run away, while others brag about it to their friends. I know of men that propose to women after they sexually assaulted them, and even got married to them. It is just a cover up in many ways.

Too many times women go through these horrible experiences and they are too ashamed to talk about it. I think it is disgraceful for any man to force himself on a woman. Some women are ashamed of an act they did not permit. Some have been slapped in the face by their offender because they refused to have sex with him.

When we look at someone with great respect, and that person turns out to be hideous, such a person should be ashamed of themselves. That kind of behavior is not acceptable. At all. Unfortunately, some men get away with such notorious behavior. In some countries, you just have to touch a woman and that is counted as sexual assault. A man sexually assaulting a woman is like a thief breaking and entering your house, taking what he wants and leaving you wounded. I don't know what other way to put it.

I was counselling a woman one day, and suddenly, she was crying uncontrollably over the subject of her being a product of her mother's rape. I spared her an extra two hours of my time listening to her as she emptied her emotions. I could tell this was something that had been eating away at this poor lady for years. I was moved with compassion, at the same time, I had to control my emotions so that I didn't end up in the pity party with her. In order to help this lady, I had to be strong.

Romans 15:1. *"We who are strong must bear the weakness of the weak and not to please ourselves."*

I realize this had taken a toll on her life. She was a broken and hurting woman that allowed this incident to keep her back from enjoying her life. I let her know that God loves her and that she is beautiful in his eyes, and that he has a great plan for her life. I let her know also, that she is not responsible for what happened with her mother, but, she is here and that she is responsible for her own happiness, and the way she handles her life.

I had to ask the Holy Spirit to guide me and give me the right words to say to her. Sad to say, but children who know that they were conceived from rape, they suffer emotionally and become withdrawn. They develop low self-esteem and show resentment, and often feel unloved. This is critical and needs to be addressed before it is too late for these children. Sometimes a woman makes excuses for a man, because she is either ashamed of what he has done to her, or she is afraid that if she reports it, her life might be in danger. Because of this, those men go free, and in their minds, think their behavior was acceptable. I'm so happy that these days more and more women are learning to defend themselves.

Chapter 45

Get Over It

It is easy to tell a person it is time to get over it when you have never walked in that person's shoes. Good or bad memories, they linger on. There are times when I look at the scar on my leg, it bothers me. Why? because in the first case it should not have been there, but all because of a doctor who was determined to experiment on my leg. Now this scar becomes a part of me. When we are emotionally bruised, nothing could erase the scar. And we'll try anything, to not have to deal with it. I tried different things to erase my scar but nothing worked. We cannot tell a person how to deal with their past, especially when we don't know what they have been through. Everyone deals with things differently. Sometimes we may think that we are helping a person that is experiencing pain, by telling them to get over it. But we are making them feel worse. Our past has a way of revisiting us when we least expect, and some of us have a hard time dealing with it. Sometimes, a person may snap at you, out of the blues, and you wonder why. One thing we must learn is that pain sometimes does not always have a face, and people's anger acts out in different ways. Sometimes God puts a person in our path so that we can help them. From the biggest to the smallest, we all need a listening ears at times. We must count it as a blessing when a hurting person comes to us for help and sees us as someone they can confide in and who will lend them a listening ear. A few years ago, I remember visiting a church, and just after the service, a lady came up to me and said, "Of all the people in the church, you are the only one I was led to to ask you to pray for my son and his family." She explained that their marriage was falling apart, and that she was worried about the children. Most of the times when I'm praying I will intercede for families. Just a few days before I met this lady, God had me interceding for this couple. When I told her that, she was so surprised. She said "Oh, that is why he led me to you." God is fully aware of everything that is happening in our lives.

If we cannot give a person good advice, then we should just listen. Sometimes, all a person wants is for someone to listen to them while they are trying to talk out what is bothering them. This is the reason why they are sharing their feelings with you in the first case. Some people are very good at pouring salt into an open wound that has not yet been healed. Some on the other hand, may mean well, because in their mind they are trying to make you feel better. At the same time, we must be careful in what we are saying to a hurting individual, because some issues are complex, and we must ask God for wisdom in dealing with these things.

> *"If any of you lack wisdom, you should ask God, who gives generously to all without finding fault, and it will be given to you."*
> *–James 1: 5*

Chapter 46

Enough is Enough

After years of trying to keep my marriage together, and being unsuccessful, I told myself it was time to get up and get out. It did not matter how much I loved my husband. One of the questions I had to ask myself was, "Does this man really love me?" I stayed in an abusive relationship for five years, when I should have taken my exit a long time before. I used to be so ashamed. I could hardly hold up my head, as all the neighbors around heard me screaming! There were times I would go in the bush and sit on a stone, crying and talking to God, asking him to please change my husband. The next question I had to ask myself was, "Is he willing to change?" I came to realize that no one can change a person. People must be willing to change on their own. When we are willing, then God gets on the job. It seemed to me that there was something overpowering this man and causing him to behave the way he did. I remember before we got married, my son was playing with the door knob, and my husband pulled his hands away from the knob so angrily, that my son fell to the concrete floor and hit his head. He was screaming. Again, it broke my heart. My son is now an adult, but whenever he complains of having a headache, it brings me back to the incident and I get concerned and wonder if that has anything to do with it.

Chapter 47

When Communication Breaks Down

Once there is a breakdown in a couple's communication, that, to me, is the first sign the relationship is breaking up. Two weeks after I got married, my husband and I were going to visit my step-uncle, who gave me away at our wedding. We decided to walk, which was over two miles from where we lived. We did not say a word to each other, because we had just had a quarrel before leaving the house. I remember telling my uncle about it, and he was quite surprised. He could not understand we just got married and had nothing to say to each other. That was a sign where the relationship was heading. Communication is the main ingredient that helps to take care of many problems. I now advise people, to keep the communication line going between them and their spouses. Especially my children.

If you love a person you want to talk with them all the time. It seems to me that courtship is more enjoyable than marriage. It could be that in courtship people communicate more. Before I was married, I remember I couldn't wait to see the man I was in love with. We were so excited to see each other, and we were always happy when we got together. We talked about everything concerning our relationship.

After we got married, we were like complete strangers. I remember a pastor said, sometimes the honey leaves the moon. I think the reason why some people never show their true colors when you just meet them, is because they don't want to scare you off. We live with a person but never know enough about them, every day we learn a little more. I could buy a new outfit at the store and keep wearing it, over and over, and never notice there was a fault somewhere hidden. Some people are great pretenders and are experts in hiding their faults, until the truth comes out.

Chapter 48

Slipping Back

It is easy for us to find ourselves slipping back into the past, and there are also times we are pulled into it. Don't worry, most of the times it is just a part of the healing process. There is a saying that the only way to overcome fear is to face it. And when our emotions, are getting out of control we ask God to take the wheel.

What I learned about self-healing, is that you must give yourself the chance to reflect on the things that hurt you the most. I was always afraid of facing them, so I kept slapping on one band aid after the next, not realizing I was only making those wounds worse. I now realized the time had come. I had to face those festering wounds. I could not pretend they were not there. Yet, it took a lot of courage to do that. I needed to inhale and exhale. I asked God why he allowed certain things to happen. Why couldn't he stop it from happening? As Reverend Ebenezer Markwei, mentioned in his book *Silver Stones for Destiny*, "Sometimes people ought to be encouraged to go ahead and weep out their yesterday."

As I began to take a peek at these wounds, the tears from my eyes flooded my heart, and I quickly slapped on the band aid again. I did that a few more times, until God gave me the strength and courage to take off those band aids, one by one, and boldly face those painful wounds. Another thing I struggled with, was forgiving myself. Some of us, if only our pillow could talk. Lots of people have pent up emotions that they need to get out, and at times, the only way is to cry it out.

Some people may look at crying as a weakness, but I realize that crying is a healing. It is a way of releasing what we are feeling on the inside and it makes us feel better. Sometimes we can lose our faith when facing difficult situations. Especially when there are more questions than answers, we begin to think, maybe I'm on the wrong track. I'm not jealous I'm not envious, I pray I go to church I pray for others and do all the right things, yet other people keep doing wrong and seem to be prospering more than me? Church people would even pass judgment and say you must be living in sin and need to repent. Wait a minute, aren't we all suppose to repent every day? What he have to understand is that Satan never gets weary of throwing punches, his aim is to weary out the people of God. Some people become so frustrated that they give into him. In Hebrews 12: 3 we read, "Considered him who endured such opposition from sinners, so that you will not grow weary and lose heart."

Chapter 49

Taking Authority

At times, the enemy tried hard to point me toward those heart-wrenching pictures of guilt, pain, disappointment and regret. I must stand my ground and take authority in Jesus' name. I will always remember what the Lord said to me that he has given me every authority over every evil of the enemy, and to spoil his prey. I let the devil know I am set free by the blood of Jesus Christ. The bible says God's word is sharper than any two-edged sword, and this is what I use to keep the enemy (devil) at length.

The word of God is the only powerful weapon that we can use against him when he come to upset our lives. We can corner him and overcome when we use prayer faith and the word. We have seen in the bible where God answered the prayer of many people that were seeking him. God knows our concerns, but at the same time he wants us to come before him and ask, as a child asks his father for something. If God sees it is beneficial for us, he will allow us to have it. He has already given us his word and authority over the enemy. We just need to exercise it.

I have preached at women's conferences, where I encouraged women to better themselves, by taking a stand and accepting who they are in Christ, using the authority that He has given them over the enemy. We always must speak the word, in season and out of season, being confident knowing that you are a child of God will put your faith to work for you. Although it is normal for a person to get discouraged, Satan love to speak lies that bring discouragement to people even believers in the word. This we know that discouragement is not from God. We must believe that God is on our side, so that we can face the enemy, as David faced Goliath.

Chapter 50

Know Your Self Worth

Knowing your self-worth is extremely important. Most women who put up with abuse, do not know their self-worth, which is sad. Some of us been told as a child that that we are not smart, we aren't worth anything and so on. So, we take what we get and think that we don't deserve better.

We women must understand that we are beautiful human beings and mothers of the Earth. I do believe in some cases, if a man doesn't respect a woman, most likely, he doesn't respect his mother. "Men drop the sperm, we carry the child." We should hold our heads high, and at the same time respect ourselves and others. No one is better than anyone else; we are all different personalities but learning to value each other is important.

I have nothing against men, except the ones that show no respect by being abusive. It is hard for me to show respect to a child molester or an assaulter of women. When we respect others, we expect the same in return. In Matthew 7:12, *"Do unto others as you would have them do unto you."* One of the problems is that some people want you to respect them, while they disrespect you. We cannot ignore the fact that there are women who also disrespect their spouses. Some women can be naggy and bossy.

That kind of attitude drives him out the door.

(Proverbs 21:19) "It is better to live in the corner of a roof, than in a house shared with a contentious woman.

A man got fed up after his wife kept nagging him on several

occasions telling him to leave, and after he left she was awfully sorry. She wanted him back, but he was afraid that the nagging would continue.

Some people overlook the faults of others, because of the love they have for them. There's a saying, "love is a blind thing." I have heard and witnessed the way some people treat their spouse it is shocking. They would not treat their pets that way. How the heck people could treat each other with such disrespect, and still expect them to lie in the same bed with them? I have a problem with that. No one should have to tolerate such disrespectful behavior.

After a time, you would get fed up, and the relationship would collapse. After all the abuse, and disrespect I put up with in my marriage, after a time I had no feelings for my husband. I remember one day he was drunk, and he spat on me. I can't tell you how I felt. What came into my mind was this man is drunk maybe he can't help what he is doing. A lot of women accept bad treatments from their spouses and make excuses for their behavior, all because they don't want to think that they are in an unhealthy relationship.

We must be careful, as some people are emotionally distraught, and looking for some place to empty their baggage. Sad to say, but I've learned from my experience that the enemy so many times disguises himself like an angel of light, just to come into our lives and wreck it. This is why we must ask God for the spirit of discernment. Also, some people get married for the wrong reasons.

Loneliness can also drive people into the wrong relationship. Some people are just looking for someone to fill that empty space in their life, so they jump at whatever opportunity presents itself without taking time to learn the person's background. The spirit of loneliness and desperation can drive a person into the arms of an assaulter, and not knowing it, until later you find out it is not what you expected. This is why we must be careful, not to allow it to control us. I remember one Sunday evening after church, I decided to stay home and do some writing while my daughter and her family went out to do some shopping. Normally, I love to be quiet when I'm concentrating, but that evening it was so quiet, that I could almost feel the fear of loneliness, so I decided to take a walk around the neighborhood. That's what I was doing when, suddenly, loneliness attacked me, and I felt like I was going insane. I never in my life felt so lonely. I called my daughter about three times and we talked for a while.

After I finished talking to her, I called my son twice, but never told him I was feeling lonely. After I finished talking with him, I kept thinking of who else to call. I remember the pastor mentioned in his sermon that "people need people, especially when they are facing problems." We need others to pray with us and support us, we should not isolate ourselves. When we do, we encourage another spirit called depression.

There are many other ways that we can deal with loneliness. First, remember you are not alone and that things can always change. Go to church, get involved in doing something worthwhile. This is a time to take care of yourself. If you need to further your education, do that. I know there are times it can be difficult to keep it together, especially when you are still recovering from a broken heart but keeping yourself busy will help you in the healing process. However, this is the time to start putting yourself first and enjoy you. In that case when the right person comes along, you will be ready for a relationship.

Some people are married and still feel lonely. I am also talking from my experience. It Sucks! But, sometimes, things change, and people change. I mentioned in this book earlier, that a few years ago I suffered from depression. It wasn't loneliness, instead, it was some unresolved issues accompanied by other things, resulting a broken heart. I've been single for many years, but I could never remember feeling lonely.

I am blessed with a wonderful family and have lots of love around me. For that I thank the Lord, and I stay focused and keep educating myself to be the best that I can be in my ministry. That Sunday, I believe the Lord was giving me a taste of what it is to be lonely, so I could better understand what loneliness can do to a person. Sometimes we overlook the spirit of loneliness in a person's life.

One lady said to me she lives alone, and her neighbor did not invite her over to her house for Christmas, so she invited herself.

God never intended for anyone to be lonely. When King David was going through a state of loneliness and depression in his life, this is what he told God.

"Turn to me and be gracious to me, for I am lonely and afflicted." (See Psalms 25:16).

In Psalms (3:3) David praises God for who he is. *"But you oh Lord, are a shield about me, my glory, and the lifter of my head."* He knew that he must rely on God to help him. David went through a lot, and got so tired waiting for a breakthrough, that he asked God, *"How long, Oh Lord? will you forget me forever?" (See Psalms 13:2)*

It is easy to get discouraged when we are praying and not seeing any results. David had to encourage himself, while talking to his soul.

(Psalms 42:5) "Why art thou cast down oh my soul? and why art thou disquieted in me? hope in the Lord for I shall yet praise Him."

David never lost hope, he continued to trust God. There are times when I feel discouraged, I speak to myself. Sometimes I give myself a pat on the back, "Barbara this too is going to pass. You are a strong woman and came this far by faith, and God is on your side." By doing that, it keeps me grounded.

My youngest grandson was diagnosed with autism after he was born, and this came as a surprise to us. We just couldn't understand why. However, we eliminated doubt and start believing and trusting God to help this child. The therapist said to his mother that he would never talk. This is not something that would put a smile on your face, but you can smile when you know that God is bigger than that. She refused to accept those words and believed that her son would talk. When he start saying a few words, we knew that hope was not going to put us to shame. I looked at her and said, "When this child starts talking we won't be able to shut him up." Guess what? Now, he is talking so much, and he can express himself so well. Sometimes I have to tell him he talks too much. One night, I dreamed he had seven keys hanging around his neck. I believe those keys represent different gifts. He is a brilliant and independent little boy who knows how to do anything you ask of him. We have seen the blessing in the testing. My son is a young man of great faith. In our prayer, he asked the Lord to give his son a chance at life and that he would be able to live a normal life. We can see every day that our prayers are being answered. We are all grateful and thank God for him and for the work he is doing and will continue to do in his life. I believe we are all in for some pleasant surprises. All to the Glory of God.

We are all fighting a battle and God wants us to stand strong and in the power of his might. We cannot fight this battle in our own strength, therefore, I am here to encourage you in the word of God. (Psalms 121) "God is our helper." As my son would say, "we must stay strong in the word and trust that it is true and real." The tougher the battle the greater the victory. If you are in a pit today, God has instructed me to take the good news to those of you that have lost hope. He wants you to know how much he loves and cares for you, and you will come out victorious.

Chapter 51

Healing is a Process Not a Product

Emotional healing is a process, not a product you can buy in the store. In the process you feel intensive pain and there are times you have to be careful how you treat the wound. When someone disrespects you and causes you pain, it evokes a lot of emotions and it can hurt you to the bones. There is no remedy for that, we must deal with it or give it to God. I had no idea I would be ministering to broken people today, I guess the Lord had to allow me to experience what it feels to be broken and then use me to help those that are broken. There's a saying experience is the greatest teacher. When others talk to me about their pain, I understand where they are coming from.

Before I was publicly affirmed to be a pastor, God had already showed me John 15: in a dream, where he ordained me to go out and bear fruits. In that chapter, it talks about the pruning part. I realized that God had to prune me, and that meant He had to trim some old habits, remove some things and people. It was alarming. If you look up the word "pruning" in the dictionary, you'll have an idea of what I'm talking about. When God wants to anoint you for his work, you experience hardship and people will hurt you, saying all manner of things about you.

I have concluded that God is God, and he will use whatever it takes to bring about his plan whether we like it or not. He could have prevented Joseph's brothers from throwing him in the pit, king Nebuchadnezzar from throwing the three Hebrew boys in the fire, and Daniel from been thrown into the lion's den. Why didn't he? I have come to realize it was all in his plan. After reading the story of Job, it left me thinking and asking questions.

I believe God wanted to prove to Satan that Job was his faithful servant. Many great men of God have given up under pressure, and we may wonder why it is God allows his children to be tested. While I don't have all the answers, one thing I know is that the anointing comes with a cost. Any person that is anointed will tell you the hell they went through. When you are going through, it means that God already highlighted you and he is taking you to another level, preparing you for greatness. People will notice you are different… Many people have said to me, that I have grown through the years. What they don't know is that growth comes with pain.

A few years ago, I had a dream that I was in church, and had difficulty standing, because the ceiling was extremely low. I believe this was an indication of my spiritual growth. In the dream the pastor was heading out, he gave me the bible and left me in charge and asked me to preach from psalms chapter 50; When I woke up from the dream, I grabbed my bible and turn to psalm 50: I read the whole scripture. It is a very interesting scripture, but at the same time frightening. It was a message that God was warning his people. I wasn't a pastor then, but there are times I used to exhort whenever the pastor asked me to. When God calls us he equips us, but at the same time, he takes us through some training, testing and examinations, and everything that goes with them for qualification. When you are in the training process God will give you some assignments. He will move you from one place to the next. Some people sit in church year after year with no growth.

I do not sit around waiting for a pastor to call me to their pulpit to preach, I believe in building my own wherever I go. I am excited to share the word of God and what he has done for me. I encourage others to trust in him, bringing hope to them in a simple way.

I have led praise and worship in a few churches. After a time, I realized that my voice couldn't carry out certain notes, and one night I had a dream that someone told me to use thyroid rinse. I knew there was something going on with my thyroid, although my yearly checkup showed that it was fine. But, taking the dream into consideration, I decided to check out the health store to see if I would find thyroid rinse, but there was nothing like that on the shelves. I found iodine, which helps to support the thyroid. I went back to the doctor and asked him to refer me to an endocrinologist, who suggested that I should have an ultrasound done. When the report came back, it showed that there were two small nodules on my thyroid and a small goiter at the front of my neck.

The endocrinologist told me I did not need any treatment, but recommended that I have a biopsy, or another ultrasound done. I dread needles, so instead, I chose the ultrasound. I love leading praise and worship, but I also needed to rest my voice, and took a break from singing. I thank God for showing me in the dream, that I needed to take care of my thyroid.

I prayed several times and asked the Lord to remove the goiter from my neck, but it was still there, until one night, I looked in the mirror and said, "But Lord, even some people in their nineties don't have necks that look like that." I laughed at the devil and lifted my eyes to the heavens and said, "Lord, it doesn't matter if you remove this goiter or not I will still praise you! Guess what? What I got up in the morning the goiter was gone! I had another ultrasound done, and the endocrinologist read the report, examined my neck, and told me everything looks fine, the nodules were quite tiny, and I have nothing to worry about. To God be all the glory! Friends what God is looking for, is a true and honest heart that will not give up, nor give in to the enemy,

But trust God in and with the situation. Just like the three Hebrews boys in the book of Daniel, the king of Babylon wanted them to bow down to his image, they refused to, and said if even our God doesn't deliver us we will still not bow! We know that nothing is impossible with God, and he could have delivered them, but for whatever reason, instead he choose to walk through the fire with them. And, they came out without a scratch. They never even smelled like they were in a fire.

That is the Awesome God we serve! There is no hopeless situation. All we must do is to trust Him, and believe that he will deliver us.

When God delivers you, it is your chance to testify. In doing so the faith of others will be stirred.

In my spare time, I volunteered at the 700 Club, the Christian Broadcasting Network in Canada, praying for broken and hurting people. The world needs us, and we need to push beyond our fears and doubts if we really want to be used by God. When He delivers you from the pit, you are going to come out shining for him. Nothing will stop you!

Chapter 52

My Vision

My vision is to help women and children, who have been sexually, emotionally and physically abused, to regain their self-esteem. Also, to help impoverished young single mothers to have a better life for themselves and their children. There are innumerable children suffering abuse every day. That sparks the fire in me to make a difference in the lives of these children. My heart of compassion would not allow me to sit back and do nothing. I also give my heart the chance to guide me into what I believe is right, and the very thing that I am passionate about. I know that I would have to come out of my comfort zone and do some pushing for me to get to where I want.

Years ago, I had a dream that I was in a building trying to get from one place to the next, and there was a whole lot of empty boxes in front of me, and I was using my right foot to push them out of the way. It was an indication that I was on the right track, but that I would face some obstacles in my endeavor. Life comes with many challenges, and whenever we want to get ahead we have to make up our minds that we will face obstacles on the way, but this is not a good reason to give up. We must keep our eyes on the goal and keep moving.

Embrace Every Opportunity

The world is filled with lots of opportunities, and there are numerous ways that we can contribute in helping others. In doing so, we too, will find joy and fulfilment. As my son always says to me, "Sometimes we must forget or put aside our problems and help someone else." I have found that one of my gifts is giving, and when I give it brings me a sense of joy and fulfillment. There are times when I give out of my own needs, and I look for nothing in return. A word of thanks goes along way. We must remember that everything on this planet belongs to the Creator, and while we are here, he expects us to serve each other. There are some people, the more they have the more they want. They could never be satisfied.

A few years ago, I was working in a picture booth at a small mall. Every evening before I signed out, I would have to make sure the pictures were securely covered. It become so frustrating, as there was a certain way the manager expected it to be done. When I couldn't get it, I would find myself crying. There were times when most of the people who worked in the mall left, and I would be sitting on the floor for over an hour trying to tuck in every bit of the cover and still couldn't get it right.

I carried my bible with me to work every morning and read it on my break. One morning the Lord showed me that the money we work for, is not for us, it is to help others. I thought of that scripture every day I went to work. I didn't think it made much sense, I thought Lord, you have seen my distress struggling with covering these pictures every evening, it is not easy, and the money is not even enough to take care of my family. On top of that someone stole my hand bag from under my desk. I reported it to the police, and they couldn't do anything about it.

I asked the Lord if this scripture was for me. Again, the Lord reminded me of his word (Matthew 6: 26-34). *"Your heavenly father takes care of the birds, are you not much more valuable than they?"* He also reminded me, that it was Him that provided the job for me, and there are some people who don't even have one. I then realized instead of complaining, I should be thankful. When we give out of the little we have, the Lord will give the increase. The apostle Paul encourages us to, "Be always thankful in all circumstances, for it is the will of God." We can also give of our time to help others in their distress. When we give willingly, to a worthy cause, the blessings will come back to us.

Chapter 53

Breaking in The Shaping

To those of us who sing this song in church, "Break Me and Mold Me," do we really understand what we are asking God to do? If we only realize what we are asking him, it would scare us to the bones, and we would keep our mouths shut. We also ask God to use us, And we have no idea what it takes. I have come to realize that for him to use anyone, or anything, it must first be broken. God at times breaks us to remove some ugly things from our lives before he molds us and shapes us into the person he wants us to be. Sometimes God puts us through the ringer and the dryer. He sets the timer to please himself and sometimes turns up the heat. It doesn't matter how much we tumble and grumble. He wants to make sure all the wrinkles and creases are ironed out. Then he shakes his head and says, "Yes, my child, now I'm ready to display you to the world."

Most of us could think about problems that we encounter in our lives that brought us closer to God. We may think that everything that happen to us is the enemy, but not always. Sometimes, God allows situations that will cause us to search for him. He wants us to have that personal relationship with him and to depend upon Him. In my brokenness, I had to search for him with my whole heart.

I remember one Sunday after church, I decided to have some quiet time with God. I'm the kind of person that always ask Him to show me my faults, so I can confess them. God knows us better than we know ourselves. In a vision that evening, while on my knees a leopard appeared in front of me. Wow! God showed me that I had many spots that I needed to work on. Another thing I was struggling with was pride. I prayed and asked him to remove pride from me. He did some weeding and some scraping, and after a time I had to say Lord, I ask you to remove pride, but please don't remove all.

I felt like God was bringing me to that place where I now had to ask myself what is going on? I had so much pride, that my next-door neighbor and I would be going to the same church and I would not ask for a ride. I would prefer to take the bus. I always preferred if someone asked me for help than I ask them. That to me is foolish pride and it can do more harm to a person than good. God had to bring me to the place of humility. Sometimes as Christians, what we look at as being humble is just foolishness.

(Proverbs 29:23) *"A man's pride will bring him low, but a humble spirit will obtain honor. For God to work in our lives we must be of a humble spirit."*

Chapter 54

Innocent Pays for The Guilt

There's an old saying the innocent pays for the guilt. But how fearful is that? There are children who got beaten and blamed for the wrong of others. Favoritism can be evil at times. We must be careful how we treat children, keeping in mind that they will grow up some day.

There are children who are pushed to the side and suffer injustice in the hands of family members. They observe in their little corner, that others are being loved and accepted, and they begin to think that something is wrong with them. Some children have to work like a slave to get a piece of food while others don't. I have heard elderly people, pronounced curses on children, and that to me, is plain ignorance. It breaks my heart to hear a grandparent telling a child, you are going to meet it up, you will not amount to anything good. Some memories cannot be easily erased.

These evil words can do a whole lot of emotional and psychological damage not only to a child, but even adults. My question is, what on earth can an innocent child do for a person to wish them evil? Can a person really hate a child to that extent and why? I remember when my son was just a little over one year and my nephew was just two. I could remember they both were playing with a little toy, and when my son took the toy away, my nephew started crying. I could see the anger on my grandmother's face as she raged at my son saying to him, boy you going to meet it up. Can you imagine someone saying those words to your innocent child, a baby? I just cannot put into words how I felt. We must be mindful that the same child that you despise is the one that some day may have to feed you a cup of tea. My son remembers at the age of eight feeding my grandmother on her sick bed before she left this world. Isn't that something?

Some children may have been through rough times in their lives, because no one had the knowledge to rebuke and cancel such curses. But, what the enemy meant for bad, God always turns it around for good. These are some of the children that God displays to the world. "Whom God bless no man curse." We have some great examples of great men like "Donnie McClurkin" "Tyler Perry" and others who shared their testimony to the world. I'm the kind of person that finds myself tearing up for me and others. When "Tyler Perry" talked about getting beaten with a vacuum cord by his father, that brought me back to the physical and psychological abuse that my son experienced as a child.

We can hear many testimonies of people who had a rough childhood. It doesn't mean when God exalts a person their emotions automatically disappear. The past has a way of revisiting us, and sometimes it only takes that one thing to trigger our emotions, and then comes the tears. After all. We are human. Some children got beaten with a belt buckle. To the people who beat upon someone else's child, how would you like for someone to ill-treat your child? I know it wouldn't go well. We must remember that God is watching. Children are innocent, and you will be the judge.

On the night of my Ordination, one of the pastors preached a message that was quite touching. The title of the message was, "After all I've been through, I am here and still standing." My son and I talked about it all the way home, and you should have seen how his face was beaming with joy and gratitude. The message stirred his emotions.

Whenever we are talking about the word of God, we both get excited. We know it is by the grace of God, we are still standing. I say it again. It is by the grace of God some of us are still standing! I know many of you are with me on this. I can hear the Amen!

And we are glad to be here. Praise the Lord!

Chapter 55

Broken in Use?

We all may think that something broken can't be of any use. And yes most of the time that is true. I remember, just a few days before Mother's Day, my granddaughter came home from school with a beautiful little plant. It was a gift that she prepared for her mother and wanted to surprise her on Mother's Day. She hid it away and waited for that special day to arrive. When it did, she was so excited! She walked toward her mother with her hands behind her back, and as she was about to present to her the little token of love, unfortunately, it fell from her hands and smashed on the floor into pieces. That certainly ruined her day.

Not only the clay pot was broken, but her little heart was broken too. She was quite upset, and she cried and cried, and asked why this had to happen. I got emotional for her and helped in picking up the pieces. I taped up the clay pot as best I could, but there was still a tiny piece that was missing from it, and it was never the same again. Somehow, we were able to use it again for the little plant, and I was hoping that at least she would feel much better.

Just like the clay pot, some people are broken, because of some bad experience they had, and are asking the question like my granddaughter, why did this have to happen? Some are trying hard to find a way to put themselves back together. They have lost their beauty because there is something missing on the inside. They walk around with sad faces, and you can see what they are feeling is now showing on the outside. God specializes in mending broken people, and for some reason, these are the people he loves to use.

Psalms 34:18 says, *"He is close to the broken hearted."*

If we can put aside our own issues and make somebody else happy, what does that tell you? That tells me, "God is in control." He is still using broken people to bless and help heal the world.

The Test of Life

Life comes with many tests. In school, students must study and prepare for a test. I'm not the kind of person that likes to sit with a book and study for hours. But, for me to do well, I must study. If I don't, I will be frustrated and chances are I may not do very well. I was walking through the park one day, and the Lord dropped this in my spirit. He said, "There are Christians who never take time to read and study the word, and when trials come, they don't know how to handle it. For this reason, they become discouraged and give up under pressure. Some failed, because they depended on their own strength, instead of depending on God's." Sometimes when the Lord puts us through a test and we fail, we have to go back and study again, because it may come around the second time. We must study the word so that when the enemy comes with temptation we can overcome.

When we study the word of God, we can shine even during the test, by his help and his grace.

One Sunday morning, while getting dressed to speak at my first ladies conference, I remember standing in front of the mirror putting a little blush on my cheek. I said, "Father are you going to let Your daughter shine today?" He said to me, "It is not only today my daughter must shine. My daughter must shine every day." I often reflect on those words, I must let my light shine every day. In Matthew 5:14 Jesus says, *"Let your light so shine before men, so that they may see your good works and glorify your father who is in heaven."* Notice this scripture. It is by our good works we bring glory to God.

It Still Hurts!

A little boy fell and hurt his knee. He asked his dad to pray for him that the pain would cease. The dad did as his son requested, and then asked his son, how do you feel? He said dad, "it still hurts." There are those of you that have been experiencing pain. It may be physical or emotional, and you been praying and hoping that it will go away, but instead, it elevates. You begin to wonder if God really cares about your feelings. Years have gone by, but, it still hurts. You are not alone. I believe that it takes the sustaining grace of Almighty God, to keep us moving even while it hurts. We all can do with a quick fix, especially when the pain can be overwhelming, but In God we trust. Sometimes he uses our pain to teach us something. Years ago, if I stubbed my toe, I would not take it very well, I would be upset. Now I've passed that stage. Although it hurts. Instead of complaining, I would say to myself this is nothing compared to the pain that my son felt when his fingers were slammed in the car door. Also, there are times when God gives us instructions that we must follow, so that we can get the help that we need. We must remember that God works in different ways. Proverbs 3:5-6 tells us, do not lean to our own understanding, but acknowledge him in all our ways.

A coworker said to me one time, that we only waste our time praying, because it doesn't do anything. And if it did, then why is there so much trouble in the world? Now this is a question that most people would ask, especially when we look at the calamity that the world is in. Can you imagine if we weren't praying at all? If we are seeking the answers to this world's problems, we need to search the scriptures. Disobedience from the garden of Eden, still reign in the hearts of us all. Jesus did what he was sent by the father to do, so that he can win us back to Him. He is not willing that any should perish, but all come to repentance.

If you are not guided by the Holy Spirit, then you will be guided by some other spirit of this world.

See (Romans 8:14) *"For all who are led by the spirit of God, are children of God." (NLT).*

It is just amazing when you yield yourself to the Holy Spirit how much he can use you to his advantage. It was the first time I preached at a Ladies Conference. Oh, what a blessing! We had a wonderful time in the presence of the Lord. I observed there were people that looked like they had it all together, but, were broken on the inside. There was a lot of weeping, and as I laid hands on people and prayed for them, they all fell under the anointing. The Holy Spirit was at work and people experienced breakthroughs.

Chapter 56

You Never Know Who Is Watching.

We never know who is watching us, and how important it is to make a difference. Having a good attitude can take you places, and people want to be around you. The day my daughter and I were packing to move to Markham, there was a lady that lived in the same building, she came to the door and asked if we were moving, and when we told her yes we were, all of a sudden she burst into tears. She said, all the good people leave the building. My daughter and I looked at each other, and we just couldn't fight our emotions. We were all in tears. We never knew how important we were to her, that she would miss us.

Just around the Christmas holiday it was freezing outside, but I was happy to take the trip from Markham back to Whitby, -- about one-hour-and-twenty-minute drive, to bring a gift for this lady and her children. I also brought gifts for a couple other people in the building, and they were quite grateful. In whatever way possible I could shine for Jesus and show his love to others, it makes me happy. I remember there was a man in a wheelchair who lived in that same building. I brought him a warm pair of socks for the winter. I hugged him and handed him his gift. He seemed a bit surprised. You should have seen his face- It was gleaming with joy. As he looked at me, trying to say thank you, he wanted to spring up from the chair to show me how grateful he was. That touched my heart.

Sometimes, these things may appear small, but some people just need to know that someone cares. It is what the Lord Jesus expects of us: not just *talking* love, but *showing* love, especially to those in need. This is how his name is glorified. The bible says (1 Corinthians 10:31) *"whatever we do, we must do it all for the glory of God."* I remember visiting a lady in the building who was in a wheel chair. One morning, I knocked on her door and asked her, "Would you like me to pray for you?" She said, "Yes! Certainly." So, I asked her what she would like me to pray for, she said she needed some onions and some hamburger helper for dinner. Okay, I said. "We'll pray for the Lord to meet those needs." After I finished praying, I said to her that I did not have money, but I was sure the Lord would provide. I was honest. I left and told her to give me a few minutes. I will be right back!"

I went down to my apartment, and the Lord said, "Just place your hands on the shelf over the coat closet. See what you find." I found four dollars and went out to buy the lady a box of hamburger helper and onions to make her dinner. I believe that money was sitting on the shelf, waiting for that special need. It is just amazing how God works.

When I got back to her apartment, I gave her the hamburger helper and the onions, and told her God is good!" She shouted, "Thank you, Jesus!" at the top of her voice. I asked her if there was anything else she wanted me to do. She said, "No, thank you very much." When I was leaving, I said to her have a nice day. While walking up the hallway, I could hear her still shouting at the top of her voice, "Thank you, Jesus!"

I thank God I was able to help in a time of need. These are the people we need to reach out to. I felt good to know that she was blessed. Sometimes just the little things, putting a smile on someone's face or giving a word of encouragement, goes a long way and is very important in our daily lives. God knows every need, and he connects us to the right people at times. We cannot afford to waste time on people or things, that would distract us from doing what He expects us to do.

My Daughter's Angel

There are still some nice people in this world. My daughter, she was seven years old at the time, came home from school with a different scarf one cold winter day. She told me it was so cold and windy, that this little old lady was walking on the other side of the road saw her struggling, she crossed over to the other side of the road where she was, took her scarf from her neck, and put it around my daughters' neck. I thought how sweet what an angel. I was truly touched by this act of compassion that this wonderful lady showed to my daughter.

This is something we'll never forget.

Chapter 57

The Thorn and the Nails

As a Christian, I use prayer and the word of God as my daily tool. I know I must yield myself to the Holy Spirit and listen for his voice. It is one of the things that thrills me the most. I lay on my bed one Sunday afternoon and decided to turn my face to the wall and talk to God, for a bit. When I was finished, I felt so relaxed, I shut my eyes, just for one second, and what I saw was quite alarming but made nothing of it. I saw a crown of thorns and three large bolted nails lying on my stomach. I asked, "What are you trying to show me Lord?" I thought he was just assuring me, that he suffered and died for me. The nails were huge, shaped like a chisel, and about five to six inches in length. The thorns were like those you see in depictions of the crucifixion.

I told a Christian lady about the vision, and she said to me it means suffering and pain, and I should pray about it. It never occurred to me that I should. Sometimes God shows us things for a reason, but with little knowledge we brush it off and take it lightly. Well, I can tell you, after that vision I experienced some fiery trials: problems, one after the next. I felt all hell had broken loose on me. I could not understand why I was going through so much at one time. In Psalms 11:5 we read that the Lord trieth the righteous. Was that God's way of building character in me? Was it all to do with God's plan for my life?

When I look back, I realize that it was the meaning of the vision. There were times I had to be brave in the face of my adversities and believe that I would overcome them, while I suffered a broken heart. I had to reflect on Psalm 31:24 where David says," *Be of good courage, and he shall strengthen your heart, all you who hope in the Lord."* In painful circumstances, many people look for an easy way out. I would not tell you that many things did not cross my mind. The enemy tries many schemes, and many thoughts of finding a way out of my situation came to mind, but I learned to rely on God. I had to believe he would not fail me.

Chapter 58

God Sent You Just in Time

I make it a habit every morning, after finishing my devotion, of asking the Lord, "What does thou have me to do today?" On one occasion, after asking that question, I was moved by the Holy Spirit to go to the third floor. I knocked on door number three. The tenant there was a lady I often met at the bus stop. She opened the door. I said, "Good morning! How are you doing today? The Lord sent me to pray for you." She opened her eyes in amazement, very surprised. She said, "Wow. I cannot believe God sent you at the right time! My daughter is taking me to Cuba in the morning for a week-long vacation, but I'm scared. I don't want to go, but she already bought the ticket. I don't know what to do. I have heard people get sick from the food."

She turned around, with both her hands up in the air, thanking God for sending me to pray for her. I knew, if God sent me to pray for her, she had nothing to worry about. I had the faith that all would be well with her and I prayed for her and told her she would have a safe trip and she would not get sick, but that she would enjoy her vacation. Two weeks later, I went to the mall, I saw the same lady, but this time at a different bus stop. I asked her how her vacation went, she told me she had a wonderful time, and that everything went well, "Praise the Lord." These are the things that encourage me in my ministry. It is a wonderful thing when we pray for people and see results, (Matthew 21:22) If you believe you will receive whatever you ask for in prayer.

Chapter 59

Spreading the Word

There are many ways we can spread the word of God.

God wants us to connect and share his love with others, and technology can make this much easier. In this world we are living in, many people, including Christians, need encouragement. The apostle Paul says, we must encourage one another, and build each other up (1Thessalonians 5:11.) We are living in a troubled world, where people have lost faith and hope. We are the ones God uses to make a difference, and We should make ourselves available to him for this purpose.

Some of us are so selfish, forgetting that the the bible says we must be our brothers keeper. We can learn a lesson from the birds and the swans how they communicate and look out for each other.

I remember, years ago I was at work taking care of the elderly, and while my client was having her nap, the Lord spoke to me about having an email ministry. I had a group of sisters that I connected with from church, by email, and I thought well, I'll name my email ministry, *Sisters Striving for Excellence.* Every morning I shared a scripture from the bible, exhort on it, and sent it to my contacts. I would encourage people to send in their prayer requests, and then I would send it on to the sisters in the group, asking them to join me in prayer according to the needs. I received many responses from people who have been blessed and they encourage me to keep up the good works.

The most important thing about my ministry, is that God gets the glory. People use social media for a whole lot of things. We have no excuse for not sharing the love of Christ. I thank God for these resources because I believe by using them, we can reach millions of people with his word.

Chapter 60

God Turns it Around for Good

What is meant for evil, God turns it around to the glory of his name. The majority of us have been through horrible experiences, where we felt like we were thrown into a pit dug for us by a relative or someone else we loved and trusted, or even a stranger who treated us like we did not belong. A perfect example of this is when Joseph's brothers plotted against him, threw him into a pit and sold him as a slave. They meant it for evil, but God turned it around for good.

I can just imagine how the brothers felt confused, after surprisingly seeing Joseph one day while they were having a conversation among themselves. They did not recognize him. (See Genesis 45:4.) I can imagine the frightening look on their faces when he confronted them, saying, "Hey, I'm Joseph. Don't you remember me? I am your brother, the one you threw in the pit." It was not easy for Joseph either. The bible says, when he thought about the experience, He went to his private room, where he broke down and wept. They all thought it was the end of Joseph when they threw him into the pit and sold him as a slave. The enemy always has a plan, but God always has a better plan.

Some of us, when we remember people we trusted and expected to treat us well, did not, our hearts are broken. When our emotions seems uncontrollable, we go to a quiet place and cry our hearts out. That's okay. Crying is healing. God will pick you up from your pit and turn your life around. According to Psalm 113 (7-8), "He will seat you with prince and princesses." While Joseph was a slave in Egypt, God prospered Him. It doesn't matter what your situation is in life, when you begin to trust God the people that meant you evil, God will surprise them. When they see you, they will wonder.

Also, while some people are thrown into a pit, there are others that have dug their own, and still expect God to bail them out. In that case you must take responsibility for your own doing. And, yes, while God is always willing to work with us, we must be willing to work with him. And that means, doing our part.

Chapter 61

Know Your Enemy

We have an enemy that comes to take up residence in our lives, if we allow it to, and that enemy is called FEAR. For years, fear held me back from accomplishing great things. It became the giant in my life, and it held me back from many great opportunities. The bible also talks about "fear as being the spirit of bondage." (See Romans 8:15). Fear overall will keep you in bondage. We all have God-given talents just waiting to be utilized, and because of the spirit of fear, we all do nothing but suffocate them. Fear is one of the tools Satan uses to torment and paralyze us, keeping us from our destiny. Low self-esteem can cause us to settle for less, and to think we do not deserve the best.

We never forget the past, as we try letting go and it seems like it keeps holding onto us, but we cannot allow it to hold us back from accomplishing great things. I had a dream a few years ago, where I was trying to climb some stairs and every time I put one foot in front the other, the stairs were taking me backwards. In the dream, I saw a tall dark man wearing a cap and holding some carpenter tools. He took my hand and led me up a different set of stairs. When I woke up, I knew exactly that the dream reflected my life.

Around that time, I was going through some difficulties. My life felt like it was going backward instead of forward. I prayed and asked God to send me help. Surprisingly, a couple of weeks later, when my daughter came to visit me, she was accompanied by a man who was identical to the man I saw in the dream. She introduced me to him and told me he was her neighbor. Interestingly, he was tall and dark in complexion and was wearing a cap. Later on, he told me he was a carpenter. Isn't that something? God answers desperate prayer. How amazing, he showed me in the dream the person he was going to send to help me. This gentleman became a good family friend, and was attracted to me, but I knew I wasn't ready to pursue a relationship, and I had to be honest with him.

Sometimes, life throws us against a wall, and we may not understand. The good news is, it is never too late to make a U-turn, but we must also be willing to shut the door on the past. It is the only way we can make it happen. Some people become comfortable where they are, all because they start believing that voice continually telling them, that there is no hope for them. Each one of us has a destiny that the enemy is trying hard to steal from us. If we don't know that, we fall for his lies and remain in the pit. God wants you out of the pit. It is not where you belong.

> *"I know the plans I have for you says the Lord, is not a plan of evil but of good to bless you prosper you and give you a good future."*
> —*Jeremiah 29:11*

Chapter 62

Finding What Works for You

What works for one person, doesn't guarantee that it will work for the other. You must try and occupy your time in something positive, that will bring you good results. Composing and writing songs is one of the things I love doing also.

It is a way of emptying my feelings at times when I need to, and also a therapy for my mind. I had an amazing dream a couple years ago, that I was in an auditorium where President Barack Obama was speaking to thousands of people. I was on the podium with him, and he gave me a notebook with a pen. I believed it must be an indication that I must keep on writing. I mentioned earlier in this book that there were times, I would take my notebook and get away to the park to write. Wherever I was, I would write. If I went to a restaurant and something came to my mind, I would write. If I did not have my notebook, I would find a piece of paper in my wallet and write. If I was on the bus, I would write on my transfer slip, so with that I decided to walk with a notebook whenever I went out.

When your heart is choked with tears, you need to talk about your feelings and sometimes write them down. Find someone to confide in. It could be a good friend, a family member, a pastor, whoever--but do not suffer in silence. Sometimes, you may need to see a counsellor. If you can afford it, then go that route. One of the reasons I decided to enroll in the Community Services program at Canadian Business College, is because I'm a person who loves to help people. In order for a person to function well, it is important for them to be mentally stable. I feed people with the word of God, with the intention that they will learn to feed themselves. The bible says we must be a hearer and doer of the word. Here is another important thing that we must remember as Christians.

(James 2:15-16) "If *a brother or sister is without clothing and in need of daily food, and one of you say to them, go in peace be warm and be filled, and you do not give them what is necessary for their body what good is that?"*

It is important for me to feed people with the word of God, but also to be sensitive to their physical needs. We cannot say that we are doing the work of God and not minister to the needy. The bible makes it quite clear, that if we shut our ears to the cry of the poor, when we cry the Lord will not hear us. Another thing I believe we should do, is to help people come out of their hideouts and be what God wants them to be. I thought the C.S.W training would be something that could tie in with my ministry and help me to serve people better. I took the challenge, and with the help of my children I was able to do it and graduate, which I thank the Lord for. Life is full of battles, and expecting the Lord to fight our battles, doesn't mean that we must sit down and allow the enemy to continue walking on our heads. As my daughter would say. "The enemy is busy, and we need to get busier."

I Needed to Recharge

After I did my placement, I was mentally drained. I felt like I was under an attack and burnt out. It was not easy listening to broken people, with all kinds of problems, crying their hearts out. My daughter put it right. She said, "We don't select the kind of people we want to work with; God is the one that does the selection. And If you are too comfortable doing God's work, then you not doing the work."

God never assigns us to an easy job, but he gives us grace and courage to get it done. When God told Joshua to go take the land, you can just imagine the fear that came upon him. God told him to be strong and courageous and that he would be with him wherever he went (Joshua 1). Jeremiah was also scared. He told the Lord he couldn't speak (Jeremiah 1:7). Jonah tried to run away, and he jumped a ship (Jonah 1:4). Moses was scared too. He was scared when God told him to go to the Pharaoh and tell him to let his people go (Exodus 3:10). Most of us may ask the question, how can we help someone with their burden when we have our own baggage? Well, it takes a whole lot of courage and a heart of compassion. We must also take care of ourselves in the process, or else we will be burnt out. The emotional energy and effort I've put out, after doing my placement I needed to recharge. I love retreats. I think it gives you the chance to get away from the stress of life, and also focus on your self. You also get to connect with other women who has the same goals. It can be quite refreshing, and I believe we all need that at some time. When God fills us, is for us to pour unto others. At the same time, we must be careful, that we don't overworked our self to the point where we can't even pick up the bible and read. It is one of Satan tricks to keep us away from the word. It is so powerful and uplifting that the minute time I pick it up and start reading, I don't want to stop. Now the difference is, we must not only read the word, but we must study the word, and fill our hearts with it, so that we can stand firm, and overcome temptation. The bible says, the word is life to all that find it, and health to all their flesh. See (Proverbs 4:20-22). Whenever we are feeling helpless, it is easier for us to sit back doing nothing, but believe me, the enemy will find work for us to do.

There is a saying idleness is the devil workshop, after all. Every one of us has some kind of emotional struggles that we are dealing with. We do not expect them to heal in a day, or by some magic wave of the wand, but through it all, God is the one we must lean on and thank Him for his sustaining power in our lives. We can rely on his grace, to go forward and stay strong. We must spend time in the Word, and stay connected, giving no place to the devil. I ask the Lord to not let me be idle- not even for one day. God has heard and answered my prayer.

(1Corinthians 15:58), The apostle Paul encourages us, *"Be steadfast and always abounding in the work of the Lord."*

This helps me to get beyond my past, and to focus on helping others. Volunteering is a good way of staying active, and a good way of building your confidence. An act of kindness and respect for others, can take you places in life. When you are looking at the television, you have the converter in your hands, you can control what you look at. If you do not like one channel, you can easily switch to another that you enjoy better. Is the same way, You can fast-forward to something that would make you feel better than being stuck in your past.

We all have the God-given ability to change our lives. We should always speak with confidence, knowing that God is on our side. Even though Satan may try to distract us with negative thoughts, we must bring those thoughts into captivity (See 2 Corinthians 10:5). We need to think and speak in a positive way.

Don't Get Comfortable

For many years, I was comfortable just having my Permanent Residence Card. I did not see the need to worry about citizenship, since my P.R card allowed me to travel to my Country and back. Until, one day a friend of mine asked me, "why don't you just apply for your citizenship after being in Canada for so many years?" And after hearing this a couple of times, I then decided to apply for it. I was already in my fifties, so I was lucky that I did not have to write the test. Some of you want to make a move in the right direction, but keep riding on the bus of procrastination, which in time ends in regrets. Sometimes all we need, is someone to push us out of our comfort zone.

Nothing in life comes easy. If you really want something, you fight for it. There are times when we have to start all over again. Writing this book is quite a challenge. I can't tell you how many times I've lost some of my writing in the process and have had to start all over again. There are times when I get so frustrated, but giving up is not an option. I'm proud of myself that even though I never made it to high school, I made it to college. I knew what I wanted, and I decided nothing was going to stop me. I wanted to help women and children that suffered abuse and people with alcohol addiction. In my search, I came across the Community Services Course, that they were offering at the Canadian Business College which covered all the above. I said Yes! this is the one.

I needed to take a few weeks' vacation to clear my head, before I could start my journey as I knew it would be a challenge. I called the airline made my reservation and went to Grenada for three weeks. This goes for anyone who wants to make the effort to achieve your goal. You may not be able to take a vacation, that's ok. But, before you can pursue and take that brave step, you must first, clear the clutter that is causing confusion in your mind.

Upon my arrival, in Grenada, I thought it was a good idea to visit one of the villages that the Lord had placed on my mind. After a couple days I called up a good friend, and I asked him if he could take me to the village. This wonderful man took time of his busy schedule and drove me to where I wanted to go. I visited one of the schools and had the opportunity to talk with the principal about my mission and vision. She gave me her contact number and occasionally I would check in with her by email.

After I left the village, I headed for the children's home in Mount Parnassus Saint George's. I wanted to get a clearer picture of how best I could contribute towards the less fortunate. I arrived there around 2 o'clock in the afternoon. I was told the children had not returned from school yet. What a joy it would have been to meet them.

Chapter 63

Kneeling at the Cross

"Kneel at the cross Jesus will meet you there."

This is a familiar hymn, to those of us who use the hymnal in church. Most religious people believe in the cross. Some kneel at the cross believing there is power in this symbol to heal them. Some wear it around their necks believing that it will bring them blessings and protection, while others believe it is a symbol of suffering. The bible made it clear that Jesus did suffer on the cross, bringing Salvation to this troubled world. It is the reason why some people look at the cross as a symbol of suffering, as well as spirituality and healing.

It is the memory of our Lord and Savior Jesus Christ and what he has accomplished for us over two thousand years ago.

(Isaiah 53: 5) *"By his stripes we are healed."*

Then we ask the question, why are so many Christians still experiencing sickness, even after they keep praying for healing? God works miracles every day. He also uses doctors and conventional medicine in the healing process.

My daughter was diagnosed with diabetes after she had her baby, which was surprising to me. I did not take it too seriously, as I thought that it would eventually go away. Instead, as time went by, it became more complex and the doctors weren't sure whether it was type two or type one. However, they decided to treat her for type two, only to find out the medication wasn't working. They did another set of tests which showed that she was type one. Now, she had to be on insulin. She went from two needles to five needles a day. This time I realized how serious diabetes could be.

I couldn't believe this was really happening. I'm the kind of person who believes that nothing is impossible with God. I told my daughter to keep a positive attitude and believe that the Lord will deliver her from diabetes. I prayed for her trusting God for good results. I asked her to meet me at the sanctuary one day, as I wanted to pray for her, that God would give her a miracle and she would not have to deal with diabetes ever again. What I'm about to say may sound silly, and some people may call this crazy. I was so desperate to see my daughter get well. I wanted her to be able to live a normal life.

There was a huge wooden cross hanging on the wall in the sanctuary, and with this hymn in mind, "Kneel at the Cross Jesus will meet you there." I told her to kneel at the cross and picture Jesus on the cross taking her suffering on him. I placed my hands on her forehead and while praying for her, I told her to picture the blood flowing out of Jesus veins unto her. Now, I know that may sound insane, doesn't it? After all, I was desperate, and desperation can drive a person to do strange things, especially when they don't know what else to do in a difficult situation. As time went by, it seems like things got worse. There were times when the blood sugar would hit the roof and the numbers would go all the way to twenty whether she ate or not. She became allergic to certain things, and now, faith was at the test.

One Sunday, I had to rush her to the emergency, as she was vomiting and had gotten so weak she could not walk. I helped her up the stairs, since she had also been experiencing cramps in her stomach a couple of weeks before. When she got to the hospital, they immediately hooked her up to an IV. The doctor said she was dehydrated from the vomiting. In a couple of hours, they transferred her to the intensive care unit. The nurses inserted needles in both her arms. When I counted, there was five to six needles, and every hour the nurse checked her blood sugar. For many days, she went hungry, as she wasn't allowed to eat. They allowed her a taste of water from a small piece of sponge, that she warbled around in her mouth for two seconds. On top of that, the nurse had to give her an injection every day in her stomach, which she said was so painful.

I looked at her and shooked my head. In all this, God gave me his peace which surpassed all understanding, that the bible talked about and I must indeed say, that he gave her his grace beyond measure. She was in pain, yet she smiled when the family visited her, and she still had a sense of humor. We could not believe how calm she was through her suffering. There were times when the nurse was about to give her a needle, and I would leave the room. I could hear her make a little scream because of the pain she was feeling. She stayed in the hospital for six days. The doctors said it was a rare case, and there was a problem that was quite severe. It was some kind of acid, dropping into her blood stream called ketoacidosis, and it seemed uncontrollable.

My sister and I prayed, and my sister asked the prayer group in her church to pray for her, as well. We all trusted God and believed my daughter would be all right, committing her completely into His hands. God placed a wonderful man in her life, and he stayed with her every day and night in the hospital and helped take care of her. He said he prayed and asked God what to do in the situation, and God told him to be strong. Even though it was painful to see her in that condition, he could not allow her to see he was hurting.

One morning, my daughter called me and told me that the acid was under control, after having an ultrasound done on her stomach. That was good news. Thank God for answering our prayers. When she was released from the hospital she was still weak. She said from her experience, from what she understands of God, it is that sometimes instead of healing he gives you the grace. You still feel the pain, but he gives you the strength to endure it. I am sure many of us can relate to that. I'm nervous when it comes to needles, something as simple as a blood test terrifies me, after having a bad experience. So, watching her hooked up to needles was quite disturbing.

One day, I asked God the same question as my daughter, if he was not healing anymore and was just giving grace instead. Sometimes, we get frustrated waiting for a miracle, but I have come to realize that we should never lose hope. God is never late. There are some things, he would just give you the grace and the strength to endure, as he gave to the apostle Paul. *(2 Corinthians 12:9).*

We were all happy she made it out of the hospital. I organized a thanksgiving dinner and invited the rest of the family, so that we could celebrate her home coming. She shared her terrifying experience with uncontrollable tears streaming down her face. At that point, our emotions were stirred, and everyone gave her a word of encouragement. We played music and danced and had a great time. I've never seen my daughter so happy. It was our way of showing God how thankful we were for answering our prayers. One week after she was released from the hospital, I was complaining to the family doctor about her, telling him how difficult it was for her to deal with type one diabetes, and her experience at the hospital, which was also painful for me. He had to remind me it was a blessing that she made it out of the intensive care. He went as far as to say a lot of people never made it out of there. Wow! it was frightening just hearing those words.

One evening I was on my way to the medical station, I saw this well-dressed gentleman he was about 5ft tall walking through the farm. I looked at him and he looked at me, he introduced himself, and said he was a farmer. I said oh yes, well maybe you might know of some kind of herb that could help cure my daughter of type one diabetes. He said to me that he didn't know of any special herb, but garlic is a good thing for diabetes. He kept staring at me with one of those smiles that you can actually read through. I smiled back at him. He said, "I can tell in your teenage years, you had a lot of boys after you." I pretended I didn't know what he was talking about, and we got into a very interesting conversation, about nature and our creator. He then sneaked in an invite, saying to me maybe one day, we should meet for coffee and continue this conversation. I smiled and said maybe. The cutest thing is when he said let us take a walk down by the dandelions let me pick you a rose. He reached over the fence handed me the rose and said something in his language that I didn't understand. He said, I love you in Italian. I said oh, and we both smiled.

I learned something a long time ago, that we should never judge people. Everyone has some kind of spiritual belief. I love when I meet someone that doesn't think I'm boring, because I can't have a conversation without involving God. I now call him my farmer friend. Every time I walk by that farm, I look for him, even though he told me that he was moving to another location. I will always remember that moment when he picked me a rose and told me he loves me. Sometimes God sends someone who represents an angel either to do something nice, or to speak a word that will help to uplift our spirit, in a difficult season, to remind us that we are important to him, and he hasn't forgotten us.

Hope for Every Situation

I believe there is hope for every situation. There are people who put their faith in other things apart from God and claimed that they got good results. Some people think praying to saint Michael brings them prosperity. I don't think it is who or what they pray to that brings them answers to their prayers. It is their faith and belief that work for them. It is the same way when we go to God in faith without doubting, and whatever we ask in Jesus' name believing, the bible says we will have it.

Nothing is impossible with God.

God did not tell us when or how he would do it, He tells us ask and it shall be given. Waiting on a miracle is never easy. The word of God tells us in Isaiah 40:31, *"Those who wait upon the Lord shall renew their strength."* Apart from grace, God also renews our strength in the wait.

(Philippians 1:6). *"And I am sure of this that he who begins a good work in you will bring it to completion at the day of Jesus Christ."* (ESV).

We must remember, we are not the only ones that suffer affliction. There are times, when I think of the innocent babies and children in the hospital. Some of them hooked up to tubes and needles fighting for their lives. I would pray for them and ask the Lord

Jesus to pass by their bedside and give them a miracle. When you can pray for others despite your own troubles, God will honor you.

It doesn't matter what you are going through and how hopeless you may feel at times, you must believe that He will not leave you nor forsake you, no matter what. He was sure working behind the scene when he brought me out from the dark pit of depression and gave me a new song. This has given me a clearer picture of how He works.

When I was nineteen, my boyfriend believed that he had control of my life, because he wrote home for me. He was physically abusive. I remember him pulling all the rollers of my hair and slapping me across my face. One night in anger, he almost ran the car over a precipice. Thank God that night Jesus took the wheel, and spoiled the plans of the enemy, or else I would not have been here today to tell the story. Every time I think of what could have happened that night I get nervous, and all I can do is say thank you Jesus with all my heart. Think about it, how many times Jesus had to take the wheel in your life, is the reason why you are still here.

Don't allow your circumstances to blind your eyes from seeing all the good that God has done for you, and where he has taken you from. He is still in control and he is working behind the scene, His plans for us all are good plans, according to his word in Jeremiah 29:11.

All the while God had a great plan for my life, but I never knew it.

"He is now using me to spread the good news of the gospel, bringing hope to the hopeless, so that they will know he is still delivering people from their pits and prisons. Maybe you find yourself trapped in a situation and feel there is no way out and that God has given up on you. He is saying to you, take your eyes off the situation, focus on Him and do not be discouraged. Out of pain and misery God will make sure he gets the glory and you will rejoice and tell the story. The bible tells us He will not share his glory with another.

I remember one morning, I decided to have a serious talk with God concerning my daughter's health situation. I said Lord, I have faith, I prayed for my daughter many times I laid hands on her, anointed her with oil believing for a miracle and nothing happened.

Is there something else that I'm missing here? I began to wonder if there was a secret to healing. I asked him if there was a secret to healing, please tell me. Suddenly, a piece of paper dropped in front of me. It was a scripture verse that I wrote months ago, and I hid it some place. "He sent his word to heal them." Wow! I knew beyond the shadow of a doubt, it was the answer to my question, and I began thanking Him for the confirmation.

One of the things we should always keep in mind, is that healing is a process. Not seeing results doesn't mean that God is not on the job. The bible tells us, *"Faith is the substance of things hope for, the evidence of things not seen."* (Hebrews11:1). God also reminded me of the two dry trees I saw at the park. All the others were blooming while these two trees were patiently waiting for their time to bloom. Two weeks later, these trees were no longer dry, they were all clothed with their beautiful green leaves. God reminded me that we all have a season of refreshing, and in the waiting period, we need to remain positive and be excited and keep thanking him for the refreshing that is coming our way. It is just amazing how He sends the right people in our lives, in the right time. My daughter met the man of her dreams shortly after she was diagnosed with type one diabetes. He was a Godsend.

Chapter 64

Respecting Each Other.

Some people are so much in the habit of disrespecting others, that they don't see anything wrong with it, and they continue to carry that bad attitude around. God wants us to show respect for each other. When we disrespect another human being, we insult our creator and grieve the Holy Spirit. We must admit when we are wrong. If we messed up we are the ones to clean up. Taking responsibilities for our own actions is what God expect us to do. The bible says that we were all made in his image and likeness. Therefore no one is better than the other. He loves us all the same. This is why he died for his creation.

Sometime back, a young lady complained to me that her boyfriend told her he does not want to be with her anymore, and that he has no respect for her. I said, "Listen, he did not die for you on the cross. Jesus died for you and he is the one you must run after." She smiled and said, "You're so right." Although some people are afraid to talk about their feelings, some on the other hand are looking for someone to talk to. If we don't get our priority straight, we allow people to continue treating us like trash. It is important that we make "Christ Top priority over anything else in our lives."

One evening while having lunch at my favorite restaurant, there was a man sitting across from me, looked quite lonely. He came over to where I was and started talking. He told me he was married, and he loved his wife so much, but she broke his heart. From what he was telling me, it seems like it was quite a while this happened, but he never really got over the fact that she left him. I guess he kept his hope up that there was a chance for reconciliation. He decided to pay her a visit one year after and found out that she had moved on with her life and was seeing another man. I can just imagine how he felt. At that point he was so disappointed, and now hope was shattered. It is not easy giving up something that you love. At the same time, if a person left you for someone else, there's a chance that they would do the same thing to the other person.

Some women, as they realize that they are getting older, they try to relive their youth. They start dressing to impress younger men, and do things for their spouse to get jealous. Some men do it as well.

Relationship to me is a technical thing. People change, and sometimes we don't even have to look for the signs. When someone says they don't love you anymore and start disrespecting you, it is not a joke. You must take it seriously and allow them to go their merry way. Sometimes people check out of a relationship long before they tell you. All the while you are trying to hold onto nothing, feeding into something that is no longer existing. It is better to be single than to be disrespected in a relationship, where the other person does not care about you. I know we can't help who we fall in love with, but if you reach the point in your life where you feel that you can't breathe without this person in your life, then you are really not taking your life seriously. Think again. When you keep running after someone who doesn't care about you, you are only wasting your energy. You should be using that energy to take care of yourself. What makes you think she or he would not leave again? These are not like the olden days. Some people are just looking for excuses to swing out and do their own thing. We often make things worse by trying to hold them back.

I Love Her too Much I Can't Let Go

My granddaughter's best friend gave her a beautiful hamster for her birthday. You should have seen the joy on her face, as it was always her dream to have one. She named her Paris, and she became the love of her life. Her mom bought her a much bigger cage, with everything she needed, but Paris escaped a few times and went missing for three days. My granddaughter cried and cried, and asked me to take her to the pet shop to buy her a fish, and I did. She wanted to fill that void, but nothing could replace her little Paris. She missed her immensely. My son is the one that would always find Paris hiding through the vent or some awkward place in the house, but this time it seemed hopeless. It was nowhere to be found. I said to my granddaughter, "I don't want you to lose hope, but I don't think you will find Paris. You'll just have to get another one." Well, I guess I made her feel worse. She said, "No, I love her too much. I can't replace her. She is like a human being. Can you replace a human being?" she asked. Those words touched my heart, and tears came to my eyes. I hugged her, and said, you are right, you cannot replace something or someone you really love. She said, "I know sometimes she disturbs my sleep when she is on the wheel, but I wish I could hear her again." This was really touching. However, my son found Paris around three o'clock in the morning, and my granddaughter was so surprised you should have seen the look on her face, but extremely happy. The mom bought her a much bigger cage just to make sure she didn't escape again. Every day, my granddaughter takes her up in her arms and tells her how much she loves her. Now she is ignoring the fish, because Paris is back. She asked the mom to take her to the vet to make sure she was all right, and she was. After a couple weeks, my son was on the search again for Paris, and found her after three days. Where there is no love, there is no strength. Examine it well. Then ask yourself these two questions. Is this worth my time? And what am I gaining out of it? You will be surprised that you can answer most of your questions.

 I use the hamster story, as it can relate to many relationships. Sometimes we want to hang on to a person and keep chasing after them in-spite of the hell they put us through. And some women don't even know they are just a second fiddle to a person that is hurting. Some people only want someone to lay their head on while they are hurting over the person who ran out, and their mind is busy at work trying to figure out a way to stop them from running out. Only to realize that you were just being used to fill a void. It is unfortunate, not knowing that sometimes people set us up, and sometimes we set ourselves up for heart breaks and disappointment.

Chapter 65

Don't Allow What's in the Rearview Mirror to Scare You

The first time I went for my road test, the examiner yelled out, "Barbara, look! There's a vehicle behind you!" Immediately I got scared and confused and my foot hit the clutch. I ended up in front of a retirement home, and there were about three seniors sitting in the yard. Thank God no one got hurt. I kept saying, "Oh my God, I'm so sorry." I guess the instructor wanted me to speed up, after making a right turn on the lights, but at the same time there were so many lanes. I was in the slow lane, and if another vehicle needed to pass, they could have always gone into another lane. I was embarrassed, and she was upset. It took me a while before I could book another road test, and I was hoping she would not be my examiner the next time around.

When I shared this experience with other people, they said maybe she wanted to frighten me. I am not sure that was her intention, but I did lose courage. Life comes with a test and sometimes we end up in a mess, but there is always hope. Gazing at the past can hold us back from moving forward in life. We allow others to come and pass us by. After a time, we need to speed up. As my daughter would say, "We can gaze back, but it should be only to see how far we have come, and to see what progress we have made going forward."

When we use all our energy carrying the load of our painful past, after a time it can do us much harm. Instead, we should be using it to work on ourselves. I know some people live with hostility because they never seek help, and cause a stink, but what good would that do to them? The best way to deal with it, is to give it over to the one who has already borne our pain and sorrow on the cross. JESUS. He understands our pain more than anyone else. By Christ's crucifixion, we were able to obtain the grace we did not deserve, to carry us through this world, of pain and suffering. Grace without measure. (See Hebrews 4:15-16. KJV). In Psalms 121, David says that his help comes from the Lord, who made the heavens and the earth. That same God is our helper.

We are all survivors. When my daughter was diagnosed with diabetes, I remember her looking to the sky and said, God you are bigger than this. We must believe in our creator and that there is no problem too big that he cannot solve. I do believe some of the things we go through in life could either brake us or make us. And, Yes, it may wound us to the point where we can become bitter or better. There are people walking through life, and you can see that bitterness written on their faces.

Those are the kind of people that scare me. Some of them don't know how to deal with their problems. When we allow the spirit of bitterness to control us, it makes it difficult for the Holy Spirit to work in our lives, and we are missing out on the favor and blessings God has for us.

(2 Peter 3:9) God is not slack concerning His promises.

Sometimes God uses a storm to rock our boats so that he can get our attention. I have experienced many storms in my life, where I felt like my boat was rocking out of control. I came to realize that God had his eyes on me even when I wandered away from him, he wanted me to know that he is the one in control. In Psalms 139, David asked God where can I go from your spirit? Where can I flee from your presence? if I make my bed in hell you are there. Also, there are times when we create problems in our lives, and we blame God for it.

When your boat is rocking out of control it is normal to panic. We must remember that Satan is a cunning foe. In the time when we are most vulnerable, he will come and try his best to seduce us and make us think that God has given up on us. Don't allow him.

The bible says he was a liar from the beginning. God gave us his word to hold onto. I'm not saying it is always easy, there are times discouragement will come. This is where it is important to hold onto the promises of God and speak it boldly to the devil. If you put your trust in Jesus and allow him to be your captain, your ship will never sink. He is still the master of the storm. When we think about his love and promises, it gives us hope and strength to rise up, go forward and do great things.

"*Nothing could separate us from the love of God.*" (See Romans 8:38-39).

Time to Shake of The Dust

For years some of you have been wallowing in self-pity. It is time to get up and shake the dust off yourself. God doesn't want us to keep sitting in self-pity. It is a trick of the enemy to make us think that there is no way out and to keep us in captivity. There are times when we are waiting on God not knowing that He is waiting on us to make the first move. I could have continued sitting in self-pity when I think of all the wrongs that people did to me. I looked back and call myself stupid, for allowing people to treat me like dung. Being nice, is what some people look at as being stupid, and feel they could take advantage of you. One of the things I have come to understand, is not all the time you have to make yourself available for people. We all have dull moments, and at times need something to lift our spirit. I encourage you to read (Isaiah 52). It is one of my favorite scripture that I meditate on whenever I need a boost. As you keep reading the words, you will find the courage and strength to get up and get out. You must believe that God has somewhere better for you, than where you are. If you don't know how important you are, let me share something with you that the Lord shared with me. Jesus says the main reason he died for you is because he loves you and you are important to him. Whenever that voice whispers in your ear that you are not good enough, think about what Jesus Christ has done for you on the cross. It will change the way you think and feel about yourself. It took me a long time to realize how important I am. After being treated like nobody, it takes a long time before you can realize that you are somebody.

Work with What You Have

You are Beautiful. We are often judged by our appearance in the way we dress, talk and walk. With that, we stress ourselves out by trying to live up to other people's expectations. Some women put so much effort into getting the right look that most of the time they become frustrated. I don't have the patience to spend an hour in front of the mirror. A good moisturizer a bit of blush and a little lip gloss is good enough for me. It takes me less than a minute. Another thing that is important to us women is having a nice hair style. There are times when I would get frustrated over my hair, but I found an easy way out. I take one of my head wraps, wrap it nicely and put on a nice pair of earrings and I'm good. I realize that is the time I get the most respect. The best person I could be is myself. That doesn't mean that I don't admire other women who wear make up and a nice hairstyle, I think, they look stunning. We get jealous of people who look like they have it altogether. What we don't know is that no one really has it altogether. Learning to work with what we have will help us to enjoy life in a simple way. Some women are pretty, but for some reason, they are still not satisfied with their looks. I have nice looking sisters, but to say I'm jealous over them, No, not at all. I love that I have nice-looking sisters. Why not? I also believe it is a good thing to complement others, it can help build a person's self-esteem. I've made friends that way. We often hear the saying, beauty is just skin deep. A person could be beautiful and have a bad attitude which takes away from their beauty. That kind of person no one wants to be around. Then there are those that shine from the inside out.

Sometimes people see us the way we see ourselves, and sometimes they don't see us the way we see ourselves. We consult the mirror and the person looking back at us we begin to look for faults. Maybe my nose is too big this is why I didn't get hired for the job, or I wish that I had hazel eyes like my friend, And there is always more that we look for to add to the list.

People don't often notice what we notice about ourselves. I can tell you something what most people notice. Your personality and your attitude, and also confidence is the key.

It is important for us to know and believe that we are not insufficient, but we are all sufficient. You already have what it takes for achievement. You are smart and have the God-given ability to do great things. If we keep doubting ourselves we would not get very far in life. You may have had some pitfalls in the past, but that doesn't make you a failure. You learn from them and move forward. The mirror is a good place to talk to yourself. I look at myself in the mirror at times and make these declarations. I am blessed and not cursed, I am beautiful and smart, everything is in the right place. Others may not look at me that way, but I believe once my nose is not where my eyes are supposed to be and my mouth is not where my ears are supposed to be, then I'm all right. It is important we make these declarations over our children too. From what we read about King David in the bible, from my imagination, I believe he was a handsome young man. He praises God for the way he created him. (Psalms 139:14) *"I praise you for I am fearfully and wonderfully made, wonderful are your works, my soul knows it right well."* We should always thank God and praise Him like David did. Children have their own struggles and insecurities. We are the ones to let them know how important and valuable they are in society. This helps to build their self-esteem and encourages them to strive for the best.

Too many times we make excuses and put limitations on ourselves. Some people become so comfortable in their situation, that they would never try to do better. There are so many opportunities and resources available to us today, that we have no excuse. We must remember, that time waits on no man. There are times when I would smack myself on the forehead and say come on girl, this is no time to waste, there's lots of work to be done. We cannot wait on people to encourage us, we must encourage ourselves. We waste a lot of time thinking about what we don't have and should have.

I believe in giving God thanks for what we already have and as we get involved in building his Kingdom, he will add more to what we have.

Chapter 66

Be A Woman Not a Woe 'man

I can just imagine when God created this lovely being and brought her unto Adam. Adam probably felt like he was dreaming. He must have went WO'man ... Is this all mine? Hey, ladies, we are beautiful! We have all it takes to cause a man to crawl on his knees. But, there is a difference between Wo and WOE. Woe is misery and distress. Some of us women can be miserable without having a reason. One man said to me that he loved having a nice woman at his side. I believe this is so with all men. There are so many things about a woman that attracts a man. Some fall in love with her figure, some her pretty face, and some her pretty eyes. I remember years ago, I was in a grocery store standing in the checkout line. I looked back and saw two guys were just staring me down, clearing their throats, playing with their chins, and all I could hear them say was WO'man ... Vital statistics. I knew they were talking about my figure. This is a compliment that I get wherever I go, but, I only remember when ever someone reminds me of it. Sometimes it takes a person to remind us of what we have, and how beautiful we are. It helps to change our perspective. The mind talks more than the mouth and works with the body. How you think at times is how you likely feel. Millions of thoughts flood our minds day after day. Some negative some positive. Let us think positive. Think well, talk well, do well and excel.

The bible tells us we need to guard our hearts, for out of it comes the issues of life. You don't have to walk around miserable feeling sorry for yourself. It is good that you praise others for the great things they have accomplished in life. How about you? Allow others to praise you too. Be that woman that stands out, that you can be proud of. I love the characteristics of the woman in Proverbs 31:30. *"Charm is deceitful, and beauty is vain, but a woman who fears the Lord she shall be praised."* In verse 10, it is said her worth is far above jewels. I urge you to read the full chapter from verse 1-31. This is the kind of woman that we women should strive to be. Behind every great man I would say there should be a great woman, and behind every great woman there should be a great man.

Beauty goes beyond just a pretty face. It is not something that you can buy in a bottle. This beauty shines from the inside out. It is more than physical attraction. When we have the Lord Jesus Christ in our lives he shines through us, and that is the beauty that we carry wherever we go. I remember sometime back, two church sisters and myself attended a luncheon in Toronto, and when we stepped into the room, we were just smiling and so happy. Some of the people commented, not about the way that we were dressed, we were just semi-formal, but that what was on the inside was reflecting on the outside. They noticed something different about us. They said to us, from the time you all walked in, you all just lit up the room. Sad to say, some people don't even know how to smile. I know this wonderful Christian lady, when she smiles you can see it's just not real. She shared with me some things that she has experienced in her life that brought depression upon her and the Lord has delivered her, but you can still see whatever it was has affected her smile.

The Lord showed me that she needed prayers. One of my gifts is interceding for others. There is a lot of single people that would love to be married. I've been riding on the single bus for many years by choice. And just because my marriage didn't work, it doesn't mean I'll discourage anyone from getting married. Everyone is different. It would be selfish of me to tell someone it is good to be single and not good to be married, which is going against the will of God, and as Paul says if you cannot contain, then it is better to be married than to burn. People burn with desire every day, and one way is with sexual desire. The bible says marriage is honorable and the bed un-defiled. If a person has an opportunity to get married, I also think they should do their research and seek the Lord to know if that's the right partner for them.

If you have a great man, stand behind him and be the wife that he would be proud of. Instead of him asking what kind of woman did I marry? He will say thank God I have the best wife. God knew what he was doing when he pulled one of Adam's ribs out and placed it into the woman that he created for him to be his helpmate. Getting married for the wrong reasons could bring you misery. I've heard of a man that was in love with two women and found himself in a pickle by marrying the one that did not love him.

Again, some people allow love to blind them from seeing the truth.

After they got married, he couldn't even touch her. Every time he touched her she would cringe. Her intention was to get the other woman jealous and make her believe that she was the one he loved. That's a cruel thing for anyone to do. The young man came to realize that she didn't love him, but that she was only using him. In a short space of time, they went their separate ways.

Another reason why some women hurry to get married, is because they become jealous when they notice that their friends are getting married, especially when they realize they are getting older. Some are afraid of being left on the shelf. Where there is no love, there is no stability in a relationship. Some people believe love grows, and I too believe that from my own experience.

However, there is no guarantee that a relationship will not go through its ups and downs, but the only way it can survive is when the two people maintain respect for each other. Another thing about marriage, if you are not sure that you are ready to tie that knot, don't walk down the aisle and say I do. If it's not secure, then when the pressure comes, and the tide rises you will have nothing to hold on to.

It is important that we commit our marriage into God's hands, and ask him for guidance, because the enemy is busy sneaking into homes and breaking up relationships. This is one of the reasons why some Christians marriages don't last. It doesn't mean because we are Christians that the enemy wouldn't try his schemes. Look what he did with Adam and Eve in their beautiful home. (Garden of Eden). We cannot be ignorant of the fact that Satan doesn't want us to be happy.

I remember giving my testimony in church and the pastor said to me "Barbara, I didn't know you went through all that." It wasn't even a third of what she heard. I can't imagine what she would say or think if she heard the rest. I don't walk around with misery on my face complaining to everyone I meet. I'm thankful to be alive and well. I keep myself occupied and do the things that make me happy and strive to do them with excellence. One of my gifts is leading people into the presence of God. The pulpit is where I overcame most of my shyness. Thank God for the Holy Spirit. The bible says in the presence of the Lord there is fullness of joy, and at his right hand there are pleasures forever more. When we forget about what is happening around us and invite the Holy Spirit in, He takes control.

The Lord Jesus did not tell us life was going to be easy, but he didn't tell us to be miserable either. He told us not to worry and to cast our burdens upon him because he cares for us.

In Philippians 4:8-9, the apostle Paul mentions, *"We are troubled on every side, yet not distressed; we are perplexed but not in despair; persecuted but not forsaken, cast down but not destroyed."*

Whatever tribulation that we are facing in life, Paul encourages us that we shouldn't give up and in all this we are more than conquerors.

Jesus knows that we will get weary at some point, and therefore he encourages us to pray and not faint. He tells us in John 16:33, *In him we might have peace, in the world we will have tribulation; but be of good cheer, he has overcome the world.*

I love this chorus. *"I feel better so much better since I lay my burden down."*

Some of us have no idea how to lay our burden down. We lay it down and before the day is over we pick it up again. If you don't allow God to take full control of the situation, you will get frustrated. When we allow him to take full control, we will then feel his peace in our hearts trusting that he will take care of it no matter what.

(Philippians 4:7) *"And the peace of God which transcends all understanding, will guard your hearts and your minds in Christ Jesus."* I give God all the Glory for where he has brought me from. Now when I look in the mirror, the woman that is now staring back at me is now a woman with a passion, a vision, and a mission. Glory to God!

CHAPTER 67

Know Your Purpose

Joyce Myers, Lisa Nichols, and others, we can learn a lot from these amazing women. We all have a story to share with the world. We are all blessed with special gifts, and every one of us have a special place in the Universe. The most important thing we must understand, is that we are here to love and serve. Some people are still trying to find out what is their purpose on earth. Sometime back I heard a Christian woman in her seventies say she didn't know what the Lord would have her do. I can't imagine how many Christians around that age are still not sure of their purpose on earth.

In the school of life everyone is prone to mistakes. We fall and get back up. You may not get it right the first time, but never talk defeat and tell yourself you can't do it. The people who knew I was in College studying to become a Community Service Worker, told me that they were proud of me. To many it was a big achievement. In order to be your best, you must be willing to get out of the mess and take a brave step. There is a true saying, "Where there is life there is hope." On the other hand, there is no life, if there is no hope. We must keep hope alive.

Another young lady I've prayed for, when she heard I was in College, she said to me that the Lord told her if I can do it, she can do it also. I'm sure that helped her to change her mindset. Sometimes people need others to motivate them. We all have the God given ability to do a lot more than we settle for. "You and I were destined for success." Because of my experience with people, I used to think that I didn't need friends. For years I lived like a turtle, just peeking out of my shell and pulling my head back in. It took me a long time to realize I could not go on like that and I needed to come out of my hideout.

If someone I know doesn't call me, I will take time from my busy schedule to call and see how they are doing, and also embrace the opportunity to pray with them. Although some people stay connected with the people they choose. We should never assume the worst. We are living in a world where people are so busy. Some working two and three jobs just to make ends meet. And because of that, it is very difficult for some people to keep connected. Some on the other hand can't be bothered, and we must be able to discern that. If you are doing all the checking in, and they do not even make the effort to send you a text to see how you are doing, what does that tell you? Then there are those people who know your number only when they need something. You would be surprised to know how many people are living like a turtle because of their experience with others.

It's Your Choice

You can choose to isolate yourself or you can come out from your hideout and show the world who you are. It is not healthy for anyone to live in isolation. Don't allow people to cause you to miss out on the important things in life. Yes, it is important for us to understand that we need people, but the right people. As my daughter would say, "The enemy wants us to think that we don't need people, because when he attacks us in a corner, we have no one to turn to." And this is quite true. This is the reason why we should stay connected to the people that care about us.

First Lady, Michelle Obama is my inspiration. These are true words of wisdom. She said, "Don't bring people into your life who weigh you down. Trust your instincts…good relationships feel good, they feel right. It is not just with someone you want to marry, it is with those you surround yourself with." I have found this to be very important.

We need to act upon these words. They are words of guidance that can save us from knocking our heads against a wall.

(Psalms 133). *"How pleasant it is for brethren to dwell together in Unity."*

Time and time again, I would exhort on this scripture, but some people hardly get it.

Chapter 68

Self-Evaluation

If everyone of us would take a self-evaluation and see where changes need to be made, then it would be the first step to improving on our relationship with God and with others. As human beings we want to be loved and accepted by others. For some people, church is the last place on their mind. Some complain that when they were experiencing hardship the church was not there for them. And we could hear all different stories. There is a saying one bad apple spoils the whole bunch. I don't believe in that. I believe that you can still find lots of good apples in the bunch. We don't have to be like everyone else. We can stand out in the crowd. Some Christians go to church every Sunday speak in tongues, but don't know how to practice love.

(1 Corinthians 13:1-13) *"If I speak in tongues of men or angels, but do not have love, I am only a resounding gong or a clanging symbol."* (NIV).

We ask the question. Why is it that some people in the world are more loving than some who professed to be Christians? This is why the bible says we should not judge anyone. There are lots of good-hearted people in the world.

1 John 4:8 *"Whoever does not love, does not know God, because God is love."* (NIV).

(2Timothy 3: 1-9) *"In the last days men shall be lovers of their own selves, being unthankful, unloving and goes on to say they will hold a form of godliness but denying the power thereof."*

Notice in this scripture below, God is speaking to the Christians. (2 Chronicles 7:14). *"If my people who are called by my name, will humble themselves, and pray and seek my face, and turn from their wicked ways, then will I hear from heaven, and forgive their sins, and will heal their land."*

This world has a whole lot of healing to do. Just imagine if every person takes this scripture seriously and do what God is telling us and expecting us to do, then the world will be a better place. I realize the best conversation I could ever have is with myself. When I lie down and relax, that is the time I get to reflect on my life, and the things and habits I need to change.

Make Use of Your Space

If we really want to experience the awesome presence of God in our lives, we don't have to wait until the Sunday to go to church and have a good time with God. There are times when we need to get away from everything and have a quiet time with the Lord. You can make use of your own little space. There is nothing like being in your own quiet little room just praising and worshipping the Lord, in total surrender to him, and he surprisingly shows up and embraces you in his loving arms. He whispers in your ears, don't worry my child, I am here, I love you. Tears of joy now flood your heart, washing away those tears of sadness. It is the most precious moment that you can ever experience. It is called intimacy with Jesus. You can have that experience right in the quietness of your home.

Don't get me wrong, I'm not saying that a person should refrain from going to church, not at all. The bible says we should not forsake our assembling together.

A friend of mine once invited me to a church call the Vineyard, everyone was talking about. That evening, I was prepared to experience what you call a personal encounter with the Lord. Unfortunately, for me it did not happen, and I left feeling disappointed and wondering why. What I learned that night, is, not all the time God works when you want him to, He just loves to surprise his children. This is just amazing what I am about to share with you. The following night, I went back to the same church as the meetings were running for a few days. This time I wasn't expecting anything different to happen from the night before. People were worshipping God and some were falling all over the place and they all broke out into uncontrollable laughter. I closed my eyes, and in the closet of my mind I begin to focus on the Lord, giving him praise and worship and telling him how much I love him. The anointing was so powerful, suddenly I found myself slain to the floor and was enveloped by a bright light. I was just laughing for over one hour. Wow! Lord! "what kind of love is this?" I asked. I remember saying, I never felt love in my life like this before. A gentleman that was sitting on the side of the pew replied, sister, that is God's love. What I experienced that night was glorious, but at the same time, it was a bit frightening.

I shared the experience with my friend, and she said, what I experienced was just one third of God's love, and can't you imagine when God is ready to lavish his love on us, can we really handle it? God deals with us on an individual level. It is important to get into that cozy place in the closet of your mind and seek the Lord. You will feel the connection in the spirit. To me it is no different to a husband and wife relationship, it is just that it is on a spiritual level. For Jesus told the Samaritan woman, that God is a spirit, and those who worship Him, must worship him in spirit and in TRUTH. Jesus enjoys when we open up our hearts to him, so that he can come in and commune with us. He already proved his love on the cross, by dying for us all. We get so busy, that we allow other things to rob him from those precious moments that he wants to have with us. We must show him how much we love him not only in church, but all through the week and wherever we are, and in what we say and do. Psalms 91:1 makes it clear to all who dwell in the secret place, of the Most High, shall abide under his shadow, and they will be protected. Constantly seeking God, will help our relationship to grow stronger with him.

(Revelation 3: 20) Jesus said, *"Behold I stand at the door and knock, if any one hears my voice and open the door, I will come in and dine* with *him."*

Chapter 69

Preparation for Exaltation

God teaches us many lessons in the pit that we can use to enlighten others (Job 33:30). The pit is just a preparation for exaltation. Although, it can be frightening, and it is a hard way of learning, one of the lessons I've learned in the pit, is the lesson of humility. Learning how to deal with pressure in the pit will make you stronger. You will come out a better person than you were before. From my experience, I had no idea that God was preparing me for Ministry. Humility comes before exaltation. In Luke Chapter 14:11 we read, "And those who humble themselves will be exalted." NIV.

When God wants to elevate you, no one can stop you, except You.

I remember having a dream a few years ago, that I was in a bible class with about seven other students and the professor was asking us questions from the bible. And when it was my turn to answer the questions, I answered them without making mistakes. He pointed to me and he said you are ready to go out now. That was the confirmation that God gave me in my dream, just after he showed me John chapter 15, that he has ordained me to go out and bear fruits. You will know the calling of God upon your life. He will show it to you through prophecy, through his servants, and through dreams and visions. God has many ways of speaking to his children.

I remember in elementary school, just before the school year ended, the students would do a test before we could be promoted to a higher class. The child that always made first place, would be skipped from one class to the next. Teachers and principals love when their students are progressing well, and always keep a close eye on the child that is most brilliant. What I've noticed though, is that teachers always have a favorite student. "The child that is slow in learning, will be looked at as being dunce." Those of you that have been underestimated by others, God will give you favors in the eyes of all those who look down on you. I came to Canada at the age of thirty-five, and with so many golden opportunities facing me, I was confused and wondering what was the best career for me to pursue. One of the beautiful things about this Country, is that there are so many great opportunities, there's no excuse to sit down doing nothing except if you are really ill and can't move. I admire people who look handicapped and still roll into work with their wheelchair. The man can hardly walk yet stands in the store front to greet the customers. God creates everyone with the ability to make a difference in this world.

I have lost interest in television because most of the time when you look at the news it's disturbing. But that doesn't say a person has to shut themselves away from the world. We, are in the world not to do like the world, as the bible says, but to be a light. We would be surprised to know the challenges that some people are facing in their lives, and yet they are learning to enjoy their life, and make a difference in the lives of others, while some of us just sit there babying our selves. If you want to know how fortunate you are, just Google different people, and you'll be surprised, and say to yourself if they can do it, what is wrong with me? And you'll be inspired. It will change the way you think about yourself. A little bit of humor goes a long way. Laughter is medicine for the heart. My grandson and granddaughter wanted to go to the store and buy some snacks. All I had was a few quarters and dimes in a small piggy bank. They said, Grandma can we have these quarters to go buy some snacks? I said, "No, I need that money. My granddaughter asked what me what I was doing with that money. I said I was saving it to buy a house. They all thought it was so funny, they couldn't help but laugh, and I myself had a good laugh. I have good fun with my family, and at times, especially when the weather is cold, my daughter will say Mom let us just jump on a plane and go to Grenada and sit on the beach and laugh.

This is one of the quotes by Nick Vujicic. He said, "To wish for change will change nothing. To make the decision to take action right now will change everything." When I look at Nick I don't see a man without limbs, I see a brave and courageous young man, living his life without limits bringing Glory to his Creator. He is a great evangelist. God is using him in a mighty way to bring hope to the hopeless. All over the world people have been blessed and encouraged. He is such an inspiration. We serve an awesome God. He is without limit. Here is my question. If we serve a God without limits, why do we put limitation on ourselves? I took a few short courses, before I could pursue a career. If you try something and it's not working for you, you can always move onto something else.

A good friend of mine stated, when people try to find out his business, he would say, "Is for them to wonder, and for him to know." You will have people wondering when they notice you are excelling. Knowing the God that we serve, he will not let his children down. He will open doors that no man is able to open, and people will start wondering and asking questions, like how on earth did you get that position? You never went to high school, you don't have the credentials, yet you are ahead of them. Romans 8:31 *"What then, can we say, in response to these things?" If God is for us, then who shall be against us?* (NIV). I mentioned that I've never been to high school, but by the grace of God, I was able to go to College. After people threw you in a pit and throw all kind of garbage on your head, they thought you would never get out. But they are in for a surprise. Maybe you were unable to make it to high school because of circumstances beyond your control. This doesn't mean you have to give up and settle for less. Each one of us are born with a gift. You need to find out what that gift is and use it to your best. In Proverbs 18:16 we read, *"A man's gift makes room for him and brings him before great men."*

Chapter 70

God is Still in Control

Have you ever wondered to yourself, why is it that bad things happen to you, even when you are doing the right thing? We know that God is in control, when we are still standing, holding, hoping, loving and happy to be in the land of the living. There are times when we must be brave even in the face of adversities and take charge. I remember one Sunday afternoon a pastor invited myself and a friend to sing at another church. I took my son along with me. He was nine years old at the time, and had just come to Canada. I was quite excited and looked forward to having a wonderful time in the presence of the Lord. Well, I guess the enemy had a plan to steal my joy, and he did it, by causing my son to get his fingers slammed in the car door. It happened as soon as we pulled up in front of the church. My friend's daughter slammed the door while my son was on his way out. Can you imagine the excruciating pain this child felt? There was no easy way of opening the door to avoid further pain. It was traumatizing.

The pastor asked for some ice to put on it, in the hope that it would keep his fingers from getting swollen. Thank God he did not lose any of his fingers. I can tell you I still have flash backs, especially whenever I or someone is closing a car door. I would cringe, like I could almost feel an effect of the pain that my son experienced that day. Again, I was on another guilt trip. I start thinking maybe if I had stayed home, my son would not have gotten his fingers locked in the car door.

There is nothing that takes place in our lives that God couldn't have prevented from happening. I remember my youngest daughter would say to me, "God would not allow a good heart to suffer." Those words brought me encouragement.

You cannot change the past, but you can change the way you look at the situation. For years some of you have been riding on the bus of regrets and taking those guilt trips that cause nothing, but emotional pain and destruction. I know you have been trying hard to let go of your past and it seems difficult, because you feel like it's holding onto you. As Bishop TD Jakes mentioned in one of his sermons that he used to think the past was holding onto him, but he came to realize that he was the one holding onto it. I thought so myself. It was a struggle and it seemed like no end, until I came to realize, the only way I could release myself from it was by making that drastic decision that would bring better results to my life. There is no reason why you should keep punishing yourself and allowing life to pass you by. You can start, by taking each day as an opportunity to condition yourself.

Maybe someone has done something that caused you great pain. You are now emotionally crippled to the point where you feel like you can't go on. People who you thought were your friend, they have disconnected themselves from you. Don't worry God sees your pain. You wouldn't have to look for connection, instead connection will be looking for you.

Colossians 3:15 Let the peace of God rule in your hearts.

Get Busy Don't Allow the Enemy

Keeping yourself busy, is one of the ways to avoid painful flashbacks. When you sit around doing nothing, that is the opportunity the enemy is waiting for, so he could drag you back down that terrible lane of painful memories, to terrorize you.

We often hear the saying that the mind is Satan's battlefield. We must use the word of God daily to detox our mind, and get rid of all the destructive thoughts that have been planted by the enemy for years. Keeping our minds under control at times seems to be the most difficult thing to do. A child of God always has to be resisting the enemy. Satan can also play tricks with your mind. It is one of the reasons why people lose their mind. Jesus makes it clear, *"The thief come to steel kill and destroy.. "But I (JESUS,) have come that they would have life more abundantly." He is talking about you and me."* I've heard people say that Christians are fearful people. My question is, if you know a thief is outside your door, what would you do? would you open the door and let him in? We cannot be ignorant and pretend that the devil is not in operation. He will aim for your most tender spot.

Jesus already tells us, that Satan is going around seeking whom he may devour. Therefore, we must be on our guard and be careful not to give him access to our lives.

There were times when I would experience painful flashbacks that provoked my emotions, and I would know it was the enemy trying to harass me. At that moment I would ask the Lord, please take my mind. It doesn't mean when God delivers you, the enemy would not try to flash those cards in your face again at some point. This is why we must switch our mind to the word of God, taking charge of our thoughts. If you don't learn to take charge, then Satan will and you will find yourself sinking into the pit again, and again. You cannot face your Goliath without arming yourself. When David faced Goliath, he had his sling with him, and he went in the name of the Lord, having the confidence that God was with him. It is the same way we must be prepared for when the enemy comes. If we have the confidence knowing that God is with us we will not back down.

All You Have to Do Is Surrender

This is a familiar hymn that we sing at church. "All to Jesus I surrender, all to Him I freely give. I will ever love and trust Him, in his presence daily live." As we know it is always easier said than done. Surrendering is not always the easiest thing for anyone to do, especially when we are indecisive and have a problem in giving up certain things. There are times we say Lord, I surrender, and still find ourselves holding onto or going back to our old habits. For us to live a productive life, we must fully surrender to Christ the things that are holding us captive.

The bible says, "Today is the day of salvation." Putting your faith in Jesus Christ and what he has done for you, will set you free. He loves us unconditionally and has proven it over two thousand years ago, by giving his life for us. "There are many people that are bound by their past, and by some force that is stronger than them that is trying to take control of their mind." Submitting to God and allowing Him to take control of our lives is the perfect thing to do.

I knew nothing about spiritual warfare, until I started experiencing spiritual growth. When you decide to go higher in Christ, you experience some things that makes you wonder if you are in the right thing. That is when the enemy tries hard to seize your mind, because he knows that it is with the mind we serve Christ.

In Mark 5:1-20 we read that Jesus cast out evil spirits from a man, and he commanded them to go into the pigs. Imagine over two thousand pigs ran down a steep hill and drowned themselves in a lake. In verse 15, we read that after Jesus cast out the demons, the man was clothed in his right mind. Jesus wants us to be in the right frame of mind, He will move any mountain for his children. He wants us to serve him, enjoy our lives and fulfill our purpose on this earth.

Every bad experience you have encountered is what God will use to turn your life around.

(Psalms 68:6) *"He leads out the prisoners singing."* This goes for some of you that are imprisoned by your past. God will give you the strength and he will lead you out with songs of deliverance.

The Drop

I remember some years ago my family and I went to to Canada's Wonderland and my daughters tricked me into going on a ride where you get into this barrel and it keeps going around. I'm a chicken when it come to rides, however it looked like fun so I eventually got in and all I remember was it started nice and slow, and then it began to pick up speed. All of a sudden the bottom dropped out and my body was glued against the wall. I was yelling out to my daughters to please get me out of there, and that I was not joking. I was mad at these girls because they were joyfully looking at their mother freaking out and they thought it was funny. They were cracking up with laughter. Then, the bottom came back up and everything calmed down. You should have seen how fast I got out of that thing. I was so mad at them, but then after I calmed down, we all hugged and laughed at the whole thing. This is exactly what God does with his children at times. Sometimes he will take us into the middle of nowhere and cause everything to drop around us. With our backs against the wall and fear gripping our hearts, we will wonder what the heck is going on, while God is just smiling because he knows the outcome. He is saying, "Don't worry my child, I got you." He promised never to leave us nor forsake us. It was a joke for that girls because they knew the outcome. They had experienced the ride before, and they knew everything was all right. Sometimes we just have to learn to relax and trust God. Knowing our life is in his hands we will overcome fearful situations.

Chapter 71
Time to Get Rid of The Crutch

Most of us are victims of abuse. Some of us experience it all. Some people have found the strength to get up and move on, while some have allowed themselves to be crippled by their past. Even if you were sexually assaulted, and brought a child into the world, although this can be very difficult to deal with, I think it is unfortunate that a child has to come into the world that way, but the real truth is, a lot of us don't know what way we came into this world. It is not something a person will go around boasting of, but, that child is a part of you, and the creator expects you to love him or her the same way. Children are of the Lord. The very fact that you have brought this baby into the world, proves you are a strong woman, and you should be proud of yourself. God has great plans for your baby. You could be raising a pastor, doctor, lawyer, a president only God knows. Give your child your best. Most important commit them to the Lord. He will take control. Get up, wipe the tears and move forward. Whatever the enemy meant for bad God always turns it around for good. The way we think can affect our lives in many different ways. If we think that we can't do better, then we will not make the effort. We all hold the keys to our own cells. Jesus says he came to set us free. It doesn't matter how you feel, there is always hope. Jesus words still stand.

Repressed anger can be dangerous as a snake. I believe it is time for you to get rid of those things that are tearing you apart and holding you back. Sometimes we don't know how capable we are until we try. Ask yourself the question, what have I to lose if I let go, and what am I gaining when I hold on? The answer is, if you let go, you have nothing to lose but much to gain. Jesus is waiting for you to give him the opportunity to make something beautiful of your broken life. He will give you the strength to get rid of those crutches only if you are willing to. It is the way you handle the situation that will determine the outcome. You can choose to let it take control of you, or you can step out of it with confidence knowing that God is with you.

Philippians 4:13 Paul says, *"I can do all things through Christ who strengthens me."*

Instead of just existing, start living. In Deuteronomy 30:19 God has given us a choice. "He commands us to choose life that not only we would live, but our children too." I believe after reading this scripture, it will stir your faith and give you hope for a bright future.

When the devil tries to flash those cards of painful memories in your face to weaken you, don't be discouraged. You may feel like your emotions begin to boil over, and sometimes you have to just let the tears roll. When he flashes those memories at me I do this simple exercise. Sit straight with your shoulders up, now inhale and exhale three times, and just say to the heavenly father, daddy, You got this. I know you have already taken care of it. I guarantee you'll feel better.

Don't you realize that we are the ones who are always in a hurry, but God never is. He does things in his own time and make sure they're done well.

Now think about it, Jesus sacrificed his life, so that we would enjoy ours. The important thing is, that by God's grace and mercies we are still here, and he has given us the opportunity to make a change. When I look back at some of the things that the Lord has saved me from, I cringe. All I can say, is thank you Jesus! And this is why I'm so grateful. I know I must serve Him. I just want to be a vessel of honor to Him. You can right now, right where you are, make the best decision of your life, and that is inviting the Lord Jesus Christ into your heart as your Lord and Savior if you haven't done so yet. You can be set free right now, from those chains that have been holding you back for years. In 1Corinthians 2:9 we read,

"Eyes has not seen, nor ear heard, neither have entered into the heart of man, the things which God have prepared for them that love him." KJV. You must believe that God has wonderful things in store for You! Don't allow another day to pass you by. Get up and shake off the shackles. Today, you could be presenting a New You!

I mentioned earlier, this is just a few chapters of my life. I am confident, that whatever situation you are facing in your life, what God has done for me, He will do for you.. And since He is the only one who sees when the heart cries, He wants to dry those tears and give you a brand-new start. My prayer for you, is that you will experience the wonders of God in your life, as you let go and allow Him to take control.

Romans 8:28 tell us we know that all things work together for good to those that love God, and are called to his purpose. Every disappointment that we face, is what the Lord uses to work out his plans for our lives. We make mistakes, but God never make a mistake. One day, I was submitting my manuscript to my publisher and my finger hit the wrong key. The computer crashed and I lost a good amount of my writing. I was surprised at how calmly I handled it. I will not tell you that I wasn't frustrated, but I never allowed it to get to me. I had already given over this manuscript to the Lord asking him to take control. I believe that it was his way of telling me, you haven't finish with that manuscript as yet, there's still something missing. Maybe, you are someone that has everything that you need in your life, but you are still feeling so unhappy, and empty. It could be an indication that something is missing on the inside. Whatever is missing in your life, The Lord wants to help you fill that void.

Life sometimes spins us in a direction that we never would understand, but as long as we keep holding onto to God's unchanging hands, It is quite possible that the next time around you could be shooting for the stars.

A friendly light
a great delight
chippered in the sky.
The morning breaks
a truth untold
mountains tumble
thunder rolls.
Birds soar high in the sky
another scroll unfold
In the midst of dawn and dew
only but just a few see the
rainbow in the sky.
Still, there's a part, that I can't see,
for God has hidden it from me.
And in his own time, when it's right,
He'll bring the missing part to light.

Barbara Ann Hayes..

www.ingramcontent.com/pod-product-compliance
Lightning Source LLC
LaVergne TN
LVHW021712060526
838200LV00050B/2629